SECRETS OF THE DEAD

SECRETS OF THE DEAD

HUGH MILLER

Foreword by Dan Chambers

BOOKS

First published in 2000 by Channel 4 Books,
an imprint of Macmillan Publishers Ltd,
25 Eccleston Place, London SW1W 9NF,
Basingstoke and Oxford.

Associated companies throughout the world.

www.macmillan.co.uk

ISBN 0 7522 7166 0

9 7 5 3 1 2 4 6 8

A CIP catalogue record for this book is available from the British Library.

Design and typesetting by Jane Coney
Colour reproduction by Aylesbury Studios
Printed in the EC

CONTENTS

PRODUCTION CREDITS

BLOOD RED ROSES

accompanies the *Secrets of the Dead* programme of the same name made by Granada Productions for Channel 4, first broadcast in 1999.

CANYON CANNIBALS

accompanies the *Secrets of the Dead* programme of the same name made by Engels Brothers Media for Channel 4, first broadcast in 1999.

THE LOST VIKINGS

accompanies the *Secrets of the Dead* programme of the same name made by Granite Film and Television Productions for Channel 4, first broadcast in 1999.

BEWITCHED

accompanies the *Secrets of the Dead* programme of the same name made by Mentorn Barraclough Carey for Channel 4, first broadcast in 2000.

THE SYPHILIS ENIGMA

accompanies the *Secrets of the Dead* programme of the same name made by Granada Productions for Channel 4, first broadcast in 2000.

FOREWORD

USING FORENSIC EVIDENCE TO shed light on history is a new science. So new, in fact, it hasn't yet got a name. There's archaeology, of course, but that's just one approach – there are many others: DNA finger-printing, ballistics testing, insect analysis, poison identification, ice-core sampling. The list is endless.

In the early stages of an investigation, it is generally unclear what forensic tests might be needed. In the case of the 'The Lost Vikings', for instance, no one knew where the clues might lead. The question was clear: how had a thriving group of about five thousand Vikings disappeared from the west coast of Greenland in less than two centuries? Were they slaugh-tered by Eskimo neighbours, killed by plague perhaps, or even abducted by pirates? The first major breakthrough came when entomologists from Sheffield University found insects on the remains of some Vikings who had died in their beds. Since the Vikings are known to have crammed people and animals into small dwellings to generate warmth, the investigators from Sheffield University expected to find warmth-loving insects on the Viking bodies. But they found the opposite: cold-loving insects. With this intriguing clue, another team headed off to investigate ice-core samples to find data on the temperature of Greenland at this time. And that led to a possible answer to the mystery (see pages 83–116).

In the case of 'The Syphilis Enigma', bodies exhumed from the graves of a Hull monastery showed clear signs of syphilis. By dating the unique wood pattern on the coffin, it transpired that some of these bodies had been buried around the 1350s – well over a hundred years before Columbus was thought to have brought syphilis to Europe. Could these people really have suffered from syphilis, when it didn't offcially exist in Britain? The only way to be certain was to analyse the bones to see if they carried syphilis DNA (see pages 149–185).

In the case of 'Canyon Cannibals', there was evidence that Anasazi Americans had practised cannibalism around a thousand years ago. So far, all the evidence had come from human bone fragments showing signs of being butchered for meat. Then came another discovery: a perfect specimen of solidified faeces. If the Anasazi had been eating each other, the evidence might well be contained in this. Chemical analysis was needed to see if metabolized human flesh was present (see pages 50–82)

The approach taken to solving historical mysteries like these is similar in many ways to that of modern-day police cases. The general principle is that any test that can shed light on the investigation should be done. Police forensic testing became properly established in the 1930s, with the birth of the FBI crime labs. But advances in forensic testing had happened long before then.

As early as the eighth century AD, the Chinese began analysing fingerprints to establish who was responsible for writing documents and making clay sculptures. Over a thousand years on, in 1784, forensic evidence was used as the basis for a prosecution in a British court: a Lancaster man was convicted of murder on the evidence of the torn edge of a wad of paper matching a remaining piece in his pocket. By the 1830s, the Bow Street Runners – the precursors of today's police force – had begun looking at flaws on bullets in an effort to trace them back to the manufacturer. From the 1930s onwards, developments in forensic science moved on apace. First there was blood typing, then saliva analysis, then sperm identification.

It wasn't until the 1980s, however, that the most powerful forensic tool of all was discovered: DNA profiling. In 1984, Alec Jeffreys, working at Leicester University, published a ground-breaking paper in the journal *Nature*, explaining how every person had a unique DNA fingerprint, which he could now produce. But this new technology had yet to be put to the test. When police in nearby Narborough were having difficulties in proving that a suspect was responsible for raping and murdering two local girls, they called in Alec Jeffreys to help with his DNA tests. To everyone's surprise, the suspect's DNA did not match the DNA of the sperm found in the victims. The suspect was innocent, and was released.

Who was the culprit? Police took blood samples from 5,000 men between the ages of thirteen and thirty in three nearby villages. Eventually they found a clear match. The culprit was twenty-seven-year-old Colin Pitchfork, who was convicted and given a life sentence. He became the first of many criminals to be caught by their DNA.

DNA has subsequently proved invaluable in investigating historical cases. It was essential, for instance, in identifying the remains of the last Russian Tsar and his family. It also revealed that an elderly woman claiming to be the Tsar's daughter Anastasia was in fact an impostor.

Someday, scientists say, it will probably be possible to develop a precise description of what someone looked like from a sample of their

DNA. This would be a tremendous breakthrough in solving crimes, making photofits far more accurate. It would also be of great value to history. The DNA of many great historical figures, like Napoleon and Ramses I, have been preserved, so it would enable precise recreation of their images. One day perhaps, the recreation of the people themselves.

Dan Chambers
Editor, *Secrets of the Dead*

INTRODUCTION

FORENSIC INVESTIGATION IN THE field of archaeology has steadily broadened and become one of the most useful and compelling developments in the modern sciences. Of course, applying the description 'forensic' to any activity nowadays is to risk an accusation of cliché-mongering. The term is widely abused, so it should be said that in the context of this book 'forensic' is used in the sense of 'suitable or analogous to pleading in court' (OED, second edition). The scientific investigations described here invite judgement; in each case the results were controversial and the arguments, pro and contra, will probably rumble on for years. The cases are no less engrossing for that, and they are presented as much for their power to intrigue as for their forensic content.

Apart from diverting and informing, the book has one other objective, which is to add detail. Each of the cases has been the subject of a television film, and while the films are absorbing presentations of their subjects, the limitations of length – approximately an hour each – impose a need for terseness, which is good for pace but often renders elements of a film less detailed than they might have been. It is hoped that the reader will find clarification of some of the complex and ingenious techniques used by scientists featured in the programmes, as well as the expansion of historical and geographical details.

The range of special skills brought to bear on the investigations is impressive, but archaeology is the mainstay. Curiously for a discipline whose name means 'ancient history generally', archaeology has a relatively short history of its own. People have probably always been interested in the artefacts and detritus of past times, but archaeology as an organized science has its origins in fifteenth-century Europe. This was a time when Greece and Rome were being eulogized and painstakingly reconstructed from their fragments by secular writers and scholars who spread the message that the classical past was a period when human life on earth had been at its best. In sixteenth-century Italy the Popes, cardinals and others who could afford it began collecting fine-quality sculptures, mosaics and other elegant works from antiquity; they even sponsored excavations to find more of the same. This technique of indiscriminate acquisition had its imitators in northern Europe, and sponsored digging for ancient treasures produced a number of specialists along the way. All of this, however, was little more than art collecting, not archaeology as we know it – the systematic study of antiquities.

In Europe in the nineteenth century, the development of scientific archaeology was initially stimulated by the discovery of the principles of uniformitarian stratigraphy, which fixes the age of a fossil by the layer it occupies below the earth. In the 1830s Charles Lyell worked hard to make stratigraphy popular, thereby nudging rationally minded people towards accepting the fact that mankind had a very long history. Archaeology was given a further boost by Lyell's book *Principles of Geology*, which Charles Darwin declared one of the two seminal works that helped form his hypotheses on evolution.

In 1859 Darwin published his *Origin of Species*. In the same year stone tools discovered by William Pengelly in the caves of south Devon and by Jacques Boucher de Perthes in the Somme Valley were used to demonstrate human antiquity. Approximate dates for the Old Stone Age were thus established; the word 'Palaeolithic' was not used, however, until 1865, when John Lubbock coined it in his book *Prehistoric Times*.

Darwin's *Origin of Species*, although controversial, strongly influenced the already developing idea of man as a creature with a much longer history that the Holy Bible ascribed to him. In addition, the spread of acceptance of the doctrine of human evolution set up a climate of enquiry, and in the last thirty years of the nineteenth century archaeology burgeoned. It took a leading role among the scientific disciplines dedicated to uncovering the whole story of humankind's development.

Earlier, Scandinavian archaeologists had postulated successive technological ages in man's past – specifically stone, bronze and iron; stratigraphy in Danish peat bogs and burial mounds confirmed the theory. In the 1850s low water levels in the Swiss lakes allowed excavation of prehistoric lake dwellings, and in those places, once again, the three-ages theory of technological development was confirmed.

In his *Prehistoric Times*, Lubbock expanded the three-age system, making it four by dividing the Stone Age into Old and New periods – Palaeolithic and Neolithic. In the closing years of the nineteenth century fine discoveries from the Palaeolithic Age were made in France and Spain; among them were specimens of sculpture and cave paintings from the Upper (later) Palaeolithic Period. It was Marcellino de Sautuola, working at Altamira in Spain between 1875 and 1880, who discovered the cave paintings. At first the experts would not believe they were Palaeolithic in origin, but when archaeologists working at Les Eyzies in France in 1900 found similar works, they and the Spanish paintings were accepted as genuine Palaeolithic artefacts, and exciting ones at that. (Similar paintings continued to be found in the twentieth century, the most celebrated in 1940 at Lascaux in France.)

In the final twenty-five years of the nineteenth century, General A. H. Pitt-Rivers's excavations of prehistoric and Roman sites at Cranborne Chase, in Dorset, established the basis of modern scientific archaeological field procedure. This was later enlarged on, again in Great Britain, by archaeologists Sir Mortimer Wheeler and Sir Cyril Fox.

During the twentieth century archaeology extended to wider areas of the world. Excavations in the 1920s at Mohenjo-Daro and Harappa, in what is now Pakistan, found the first evidence of the prehistoric Indus civilization. Later excavations in eastern China proved that there had been a prehistoric Chinese culture that could be identified with the Shang dynasty, previously known only through references to it in early Chinese records.

The twentieth century saw an increase in archaeological knowledge of prehistoric times in the New World: one notable advance was the discovery of the origin of domesticated crops in Central America; another was the locating of the remains of the Olmec civilization of Mexico, dating from 1000 to 300 BC. The Olmec were the oldest of the New World civilizations and are considered to be the parent of all the others.

The vast growth of archaeology and its increasing importance in commerce and industry has led to its being established as an academic discipline, and no university of any importance lacks a department of archaeology staffed by enthusiastic specialists. The forensic persuasion within the profession – whose work this book aims to illuminate – grows apace. Forensic specialists employ a dazzling range of subsidiary and supplementary skills to answer specialized questions about our own and our planet's past, and they do so in increasingly fine detail. Nowadays, the wide literature of archaeology is augmented by dozens of journals in many languages as well as many books and magazines aimed at spanning the divide between professionals and lay enthusiasts. Archaeology has come of age and continues to gain strength in the forefront of the sciences.

The investigations presented here have a lot in common, notably the fact that they explore humanity's past to find answers that change our view of history. But although there are shared features, there is no shortage of variety. The reader is taken to a bleak moor in the north of England where archaeologists and bone specialists uncover the shocking truth of the most bloody and appalling one-day battle in medieval English history; then off to the American South-West, where human bones and fossilized excrement are the keys to the discovery of cannibalism among early native Americans. In locations as far apart as England, America and Spain, ancient evidence is sifted and argued over by experts keen to determine the origins of syphilis, while in Greenland international scientists of several disciplines use their ingenuity to discover why, in the fourteenth century, the residents of a Viking settlement simply disappeared. Superstition, psychology and the mysteries of plant pharmacology have a look-in, too, when an American investigator makes startling revelations about a plague that wiped out half the population of Europe in the fourteenth century, and another proposes a previously unsuspected cause of 'hysteria' in the girls who set off the notorious witch trials in Salem, Massachusetts, in 1692.

'The proper study of mankind is man,' wrote Alexander Pope, and who would quarrel with that? By knowing ourselves, we encompass most of what is worth knowing. Thanks to the quality of enquiry disclosed in these pages, our knowledge grows wider every hour.

Hugh Miller

1

BLOOD RED ROSES

THE FIGHTING HAD BEEN over for centuries before M. Graham, a children's author writing in 1835, coined the phrase 'Wars of the Roses' to describe the civil wars that raged in England between 1455 and 1485. The 'roses' were the heraldic emblems of rival branches of the House of Plantagenet: a white rose for the Yorkists, a red rose for the Lancastrians. As the years of fighting wore on and the battles degenerated into slaughter on a savage scale, the roses came to symbolize the decline of chivalry. 'The red rose might become white,' wrote the clergyman and author Thomas Fuller, 'by losing so much blood, and the white rose red by shedding it.'

Wholesale carnage reached its peak at a battle fought near the Yorkshire village of Towton on 29 March 1461. Greater numbers were engaged that day, and more men killed, than in any other battle of the Wars of the Roses. Five hundred years later, archaeologists uncovered evidence of how as many as 28,000 men may have met their deaths that day.

To gain some idea of the level of bad blood between the Yorkists and the Lancastrians, it helps to know something of the events leading up to the Battle of Towton. The Wars of the Roses had their roots in the final months of the fourteenth century, when Henry Bolingbroke of the House of Lancaster overthrew Richard II and had himself crowned Henry IV. Twenty-three years later his son, Henry V, would die at the age of thirty-five and be succeeded by his only child, also named Henry, who was proclaimed king while he was still a baby. Henry V had been the victor at Agincourt, one of a drawn-out series of battles between England and France which would eventually be labelled the Hundred Years War. The fighting carried on into the reign of Henry VI, finally petering out in 1453, by which time it had seriously undermined England's wealth and manpower. The royal fortune, too, was all but drained away, and as matters grew worse the king, a man with no taste or talent for government, became more and more reclusive. The situation at court was not helped by the fact that the queen, Margaret of Anjou, was a scheming, domineering woman who completely overshadowed her husband.

In August 1453 Henry went temporarily insane. For eighteen months he was completely disorientated and incapable of identifying his surroundings. In the meantime Queen Margaret produced an heir, Edward, and made vigorous representations to Parliament, asking that she be made regent. In France there was a precedent for such a move, but this was not the case in England. A powerful baronial clique headed by Richard Neville, Earl of Warwick – the 'Kingmaker' and a staunch Yorkist – rejected the queen's request and installed Richard, Duke of York, as 'protector' of the realm.

When eventually Henry had recovered sufficiently to take the throne again, he imediately proclaimed his support for Queen Margaret and her adherents. York, seeing his position of strength threatened by this, took up arms and directly challenged the king's authority.

The House of York was now in direct conflict with the House of Lancaster. The first battle of the Wars of the Roses was fought at St Albans on 22 May 1455. It resulted in a Yorkist victory, and there followed four years of fragile truce.

Civil war broke out again in 1459. The Yorkists succeeded on 23 September, but they were routed in a skirmish on 12 October. In France the Earl of Warwick reassembled the Yorkist forces, and in June 1460 he came back to England, where he defeated the Lancastrians at Northampton. At that point York tried to claim the Crown, but the lords in Parliament were reluctant to undo the precedents of the preceding seventy years, which effectively would have cancelled all that had been done since the Lancastrians came to power. A compromise was reached, and York settled for the right to become king when Henry died. This ruling disinherited Henry's only son, Prince Edward, and intensified Queen Margaret's opposition to York. She withdrew to Hull and worked hard at establishing alliances with the northern lords and the Scots.

In the winter of 1460 Margaret's troops harassed a number of the Duke of York's tenants on his Yorkshire estates. York went to their defence, and during a Christmas truce he sheltered with his troops at Sandal Castle in Wakefield. On 30 December, having been lured from the castle, the Yorkists were ambushed and the duke was killed, along with his seventeen-year-old son, Edmund. The Lancastrians cut off York's head, crowned it with paper and stuck it on a pike at Micklegate in York.

Queen Margaret now marched south towards London. Meanwhile, the title of Duke of York passed to the dead duke's eighteen-year-old heir, Edward, a precocious campaigner who defeated a Lancastrian force at Mortimer's Cross, Herefordshire, a month after he took the title in 1461.

The Yorkist alliance under Warwick headed for London, but its troops were defeated by Margaret's army at the second Battle of St Albans.

Margaret had intended to enter London and hold it, but she was losing men through desertion, so instead she and her army turned north, surviving by plunder as they went. This was a relief for the people of London, who were fearful of Margaret and her army. As a contemporary chronicler wrote:

> All this season was great watch kept in the city of London
> for it was reported that the queen with the northern men
> would come down to the city and rob and despoil the city
> and destroy it utterly and all the south country.

On 4 March the young Duke of York was 'elected' King Edward IV by the citizens of London. His first act as king was to send Warwick north with a massive army to pursue Margaret. Delaying only long enough to set the Duke of Norfolk the task of recruiting more men for the Yorkist cause, the king himself then headed north.

Days later the Yorkist and Lancastrian armies forgathered to do battle sixteen kilometres south-west of York at a place called Towton.

In August 1996, during building work for an extension at Towton Hall, workmen accidentally disturbed a burial pit containing several human skeletons. The North Yorkshire County Council Heritage Unit asked archaeologists and bone specialists from the University of Bradford to help recover the remains from the pit.

'It was a unique experience in that we had never excavated a mass grave before,' said Malin Holst, a bone specialist. 'I think very few people have, so it was exciting from that point of view. It was a big challenge as well.'

Exhuming the bones would be no straightforward matter. Expensive building work had to be put on hold, which meant the archaeologists had very little time; even so, they would have to work with extraordinary care, because the fragile skeletons lay compressed in a grave measuring 6 metres by 2 metres by only 50 centimetres deep.

'At the initial stage we didn't quite realize how little time we would have,' Malin Holst explained. 'We didn't know the size of the grave, either, so at first we uncovered the top, which turned out to be rectangular in shape.'

They uncovered the first skeleton by carefully cleaning the soil from around it. That was when they began to see the other skeletons directly underneath. A strategy had to be developed which would prevent any of them standing or kneeling on the skeletons and possibly destroying them. They decided to use planks that they rested on the edges of the trench and from which they were able to work downwards. Then they proceeded to one skeleton at a time or, when it was possible, several at once. As Malin Holst explained:

> When the soil was removed from them, they were photographed in situ. Sketches of them were made, and they were surveyed so we would have an exact location of each skeleton in the grave. It was only once that was done that we lifted them out of the grave, bone by bone. In a mass burial there are so many different individuals, of course. You really need to know a lot about bones to be able to excavate a skeleton successfully under those conditions. A lot of the arm bones were lying next to each other, so we had to really make sure what belonged to whom.

Even before the exhumation was complete, it was clear from the appearance of some skulls that these men had died violently. 'I think a lot of people have a very romantic view of medieval warfare,' said Malin. 'The injuries we found at Towton really brought these people to life and showed what they must have undergone. They gave us a picture that isn't romantic at all. They showed us a very horrific death.'

Before the bones could be retrieved, it was important to map their positions in the cramped pit. First, superficial debris was carefully removed. An infra-red theodolite was then used to establish a network of fixed reference points on the skeletons, in the same way that surveyors pinpoint landmarks when making maps and site layouts. The accumulated electronic data was fed automatically to a computer inside the theodolite, and the computer organized and stored the data as three-dimensional co-ordinates. These, in their turn, could be read and interpreted by computer-aided design software.

'We surveyed sixteen points on each body,' noted Tim Sutherland, an archaeologist; 'one point on the centre of the skull, one on each shoulder, one on each elbow, one on each wrist, three down the spine and three down each leg.' The surveyed data from the skeletons was used to create a three-dimensional computer graphic of the 500-year-old tableau in the pit, accurately showing the layering of the bones and their relative positions to within an accuracy of a millimetre.

'One has to imagine that this was a very fierce battle,' remarked Malin Holst. 'As many people as possible had to be buried in the shortest possible time and in very unfavourable conditions. The soldiers were packed carelessly in the grave. Little spaces had been used to fit people in any way they could, and there was very, very tight layering.'

There were thirty-seven skeletons in all. As they were carefully removed and boxed, it was noted that the grave contained no traces of metal or leather. This suggested that the victims had been stripped naked. The only item of personal property to come out of the pit was a small silver finger ring.

'Once we got to the lab,' Malin said, 'we proceeded to clean all the dirt off each individual. In most cases we knew what belonged to whom, but when we didn't know we tried to match individual bones to whole skeletons, and this we did by studying bone structure – for example, how pronounced the muscle attachments were for a certain individual; also the colour of the bone. With the skulls it was more difficult, because we had tiny pieces that we had to fit and glue together, a very time-consuming process.'

Because people experienced in bone exhumation had been at the burial site, the skeletons had been retrieved with a high level of professional care. A sound working knowledge of osteology (the scientific study of bones) had been absolutely crucial, too, as Malin confirmed: 'We actually had almost every one of the skeletons complete, even though they were fragmentary. I don't think that would have been possible if the people on site hadn't been trained in osteology.'

The bone specialists' first investigative task was to determine the approximate age of the individuals at the time they died. Estimating age from bones calls for considerable patience and a degree of judgement that comes only with experience. Although growth-changes in the skeleton provide a reliable basis for assessing age, they don't allow an exact determination, since so many variations between individuals can be attributed to growth, nutrition and heredity.

Before puberty, when the skeleton begins to toughen and many growth-changes are taking place – including the development of the ends of the limb bones, and the progressive hardening and eruption of the teeth – it is comparatively easy to determine age to within a year or so.

From puberty until the consolidation of the skeleton, a fairly close estimate can still be made to within a range of two to three years: this is done by noting the progress of the joining up of the epiphyses, which are small parts of bone separated from the main body of the bone by a layer of cartilage. These become united with the bone at any time from the twenty-second to the twenty-fifth year. So when all the little epiphyses of the limb bones are completely united to their main bones, it can be assumed that the subject's minimum age was twenty-two years, at the most twenty-five. After that, the estimation range has to lengthen, and beyond thirty years, when the mature skeleton already begins to show signs of ageing, it is hardly safe to estimate more closely than in decades.

But even after apparent adulthood has been reached, and particularly towards later adult life, indications of age can still be detected in the bones. For example, the absence of closure of any of the skull sutures (the sutures are the jagged margin lines between the bones of the head) makes it probable that the deceased was no more than thirty years old. The closure of three of the sutures – namely the sagittal, coronal and lambdoid – has usually begun by the age of thirty. The two sutures called the parieto-mastoid and the squamous start to close up between the ages of thirty-five and forty but don't show any great advancement of the closure until between fifty and sixty. The remaining suture, called the spheno-parietal, begins to close at thirty but is not usually completely closed until about the age of seventy.

Work on age-estimation from bones is unending, and nowadays researchers have a vast accumulation of procedures and techniques to call on. Much of the skill of the investigators on the Bradford team lay in their ability not only to draw on accumulated knowledge and experience but to know which strategies were best suited to the cases in hand.

Examination of the skulls and other bones from Towton revealed that the dead were men and boys ranging in age from sixteen to fifty. Carbon dating was used to find out when they had died. The procedure, properly called radiocarbon dating, determines the age of organic matter by measuring the amount of radioactive decay in its structure. All living things contain the radiocarbon called carbon-14. On the death of an organism, the amount of carbon-14 in its structure begins to decrease at a steady rate. Since the half-life of carbon-14 (half-life means the time it takes for half the material to decay) is known to be 5,730 years, an estimate of the date at which a human being or other organism died can be made by measuring the amount of carbon-14 in its remains. In the case of the Towton warriors, carbon dating of the bones confirmed they had died at the time of the battle. The cause of death was obvious from their terrible head wounds. Malin Holst remarked that at first it was hard to believe the horrendous extent of the wounding. But the evidence was there in front of her, stark and undeniable. 'One of the individuals had thirteen skull injuries. It seemed almost inhuman, *unnatural*, for anybody to be hacked to death in such a way.'

Medieval war was never a civilized affair, but the extent of the wounding found on the men at Towton suggested unusual viciousness on the part of their attackers. David Edge, Curator of Arms and Armour at the Wallace Collection in London, pointed out that Edward IV did not travel north in a sunny frame of mind:

> Eighteen-year-old Edward, he's lost his father, he's lost his seventeen-year-old brother … Is he going to arrive at the Battle of Towton three months later full of the milk of human kindness, with a forgiving nature? No. What he's out for is vengeance. He wants the murderers of his family. I think the scene is set for a particularly brutal and vicious conflict.

In the turmoil and confusion of civil war, many formal records disappeared, and for evidence of the ferocity of the fighting at Towton we have to rely on contemporary chronicles and handed-down accounts. We are told that the Lancastrians had superior numbers and were first to reach the battlefield from their encampment at York. The ground they chose, south of Tadcaster, was the highest point between Pontefract and York, a limestone plateau thirty metres above the surrounding land and overlooking the main road north.

The Yorkists reached Pontefract on 27 March. Early next morning they sent a small unit of men to erect and guard a temporary bridge over the River Aire. The Lancastrians took the bridge by force, causing the Yorkists to come north in strength to win it back. The skirmish produced heavy casualties on both sides.

On the night before the big battle the Yorkists, unlike the main Lancastrian force, had no shelter and precious few supplies. They camped in the open in the freezing March winds. 'With snow and ice,' an observer wrote, 'it was pitiful to see men and horses suffer.'

As Palm Sunday dawned, both sides took up their battle positions, confronting each other across what was effectively a shallow valley, with the Lancastrians facing south from the higher ground. The Yorkists had fewer troops, but they had the weather on their side. At dawn, snow and sleet were blowing a blizzard into the Lancastrians' faces.

Andrew Boardman, an authority on the Battle of Towton, believes both sides set their archers – thousands of them – at the front, probably in a chequerboard formation, allowing space for each man to manoeuvre his bow. Behind the archers were the main van of armoured fighters, all on foot, and to their rear were light horsemen and reserves with lances and spikes.

According to Edward Hall, a Tudor chronicler who documented the battle, a great shout went up from both sides as the armies faced each other. Andrew Boardman described the opening of the battle:

Orders of 'no quarter' passed around the armies, and they took the field. The vanguard came on first, protecting the rearguard and the mainguard. The Yorkist bowmen went forward under cover of the snow and shot a volley into the ranks of the Lancastrians. If the snow was as bad as I've sometimes seen it on that plateau, then visibility was very, very poor. The Lancastrians shot back, but their arrows fell short of the Yorkist ranks. All the Yorkists did was pick up the arrows and shoot them back. They kept doing this for a considerable length of time.

Each longbowman had about forty-eight arrows in his quiver. Boardman estimates that if the Yorkist bowmen used all their arrows, plus those they picked up and fired back at the Lancastrians, each man probably fired about a hundred arrows. 'If you take a hundred arrows and multiply that by the number of men in the Yorkist vanguard, then you've got about a million arrows – and that's about forty tonnes. So it was probably the biggest exchange of arrows in British history.'

The tactic of putting in a volley under cover of the weather had proved incredibly fortunate for the Yorkists. It gave them a lead by causing the first heavy casualties of the battle; because the Lancastrians couldn't hit back, and because they inadvertently provided the Yorkists with more ammunition to keep up the assault, the casualty list became grotesquely one-sided. As Boardman explained:

I guess a lot of people have the wrong idea about a medieval battle. They imagine there were knights in shiny armour and that it was all brightness and there were banners flying, and they'd start at nine o'clock and decide that they would finish as soon as a certain number of casualties had been incurred. But the reality of it was like all wars – brutal. Medieval battle was the worst kind of slaughter because it was hand-to-hand, killing up close.

The fighting is said to have lasted ten hours with hundreds, even thousands of close-quarter battles between small units within the mass of fighting men. Considering the kind of weaponry the combatants used, the most horrific injuries must have been inflicted. Most of the nobility would have carried two-handed pole-axes – very heavy weapons, 190 centimetres long with massive honed blades. The common soldier would carry a halberd or a billhook. A halberd is a shafted weapon with an axe-like cutting blade, a sharp steel beak and an apical spike. Billhooks were more common; probably every house in a village had a bill at the side of the door, ready to deal with intruders or any other serious trouble, so most men could pick one up and fight with it. Billhooks were long-handled weapons, much longer than pole-axes, with massive heads fitted with spikes and hooking implements designed to unseat cavalrymen from their saddles and jerk infantrymen's legs from under them. For a defensive weapon, the ordinary longbowman had an axe with a maul, or hammer-head, used for killing and for driving in stakes. There was protective armour of variable efficiency, but, as Boardman pointed out, it was rarely government-issue:

Enforcing the Statute of Winchester, which was a statute requiring all able-bodied men between the ages of sixteen and sixty to fight for their king, the commissioners went on recruiting drives round the villages and towns. The men they pulled into service were required by law to have some form of basic armour. If for any reason the gear wasn't already in their possession, then the town would have to provide it.

As the day wore on at Towton, the balance began to shift. In spite of their casualties, the Lancastrians managed to push the Yorkists back across the southern plateau and, coming out on the far west of the battlefield, ambushed their flank. 'All the while, it snew,' wrote Edward Hall, the chronicler.

By early afternoon the Yorkists were seriously losing ground. Their position was suddenly reversed, however, by the arrival of reinforcements recruited by the Duke of Norfolk. The fresh troops came up the north road and on to the plateau to attack the Lancastrians' eastern flank. It was a surprise assault by fit men in such numbers that they overwhelmed the Lancastrians and threw them into disorder.

The Lancastrians' fighting unity collapsed. They broke ranks and ran for their lives. Fleeing soldiers tried to escape down the trough of Towton Dale, towards the marshes or straight over the steep western edge of the plateau towards Cock Beck, a nearby river. The open land known as North Acres and the slopes of the dale were easy territory for cavalry to slash, stick and spear the escaping soldiers. A tight throng of Lancastrians tried to wade across Cock Beck, but although narrow it was deep and cold. According to another chronicler, a large number of exhausted, terrified men in heavy kit drowned, making it possible for the living to cross on a bridge of corpses. The crossing, though, was no escape. The Yorkists chased fleeing Lancastrians right into the streets of Tadcaster, killing many of them there.

What facts could the burial pit offer the archaeologists? For a start, the skeletons were a broad mix of body types, ranging in height from 160 to 182 centimetres; the average height of an English adult male of that period was 171.8 centimetres. They were fighting men, although there was no way of knowing whose side they had been on. As Chris Knusel, a biological anthropologist on the University of Bradford team, explained:

> I think we have individuals from almost every walk of medieval life. I say that because of the variety in their general stature, which suggests they were drawn from a whole range of lifestyles. Some individuals bear previous injuries, suggesting a very strenuous style of living, while others are no different from the ordinary medieval population.

Because the archaeologists had been able to recover whole skeletons, they could begin to work out the physique of individual bodies. 'It was very fortunate that we had complete individuals to work with,' said Malin Holst. 'A complete skeleton gave us a fuller picture of what a person went through. We were able to work out that some of them were very strongly developed; others might have had dietary deficiencies. Quite a number of individuals showed greater development in their left arms than in their right, which could indicate they had been practising archery' on the medieval battlefield.

Only ten per cent of those on the medieval battlefield were knights in armour; the rest were foot soldiers, most of them conscripts. In English armies, the archers were the backbone of this infantry, and the longbow was their weapon of mass destruction. Practice with the bow was enforced by law, and had produced a breed of men with formidable killing power. Matthew Bennett of the Royal Military Academy, Sandhurst, explained:

> If there was one glory of English arms in the late Middle Ages, it was the bowman. Edward I used large numbers of

archers in the late thirteenth century, and by the time of Edward III, in the mid-fourteenth century, English archers were going abroad. There was plenty to be gained in French campaigns – great victories like Agincourt would make an archer a rich man.

In the course of the Hundred Years War, English archers became the most feared and lethally efficient soldiers of the age. 'During most of those battles, the French were outshot by ordinary Englishmen and Welshmen,' said Simon Stanley, an expert bowman and an authority on archery. 'The difference between the English and French tactics was that the English had masses of archers but the French had only a few, and the ones they had were not trained to the same levels of skill as the English. The nobility and ruling powers in France did not want to have their ordinary peasants armed with the longbow in case they got a revolution on their hands.'

The archers at the Battle of Towton were the sons and grandsons of the generation that fought at Agincourt, so they were men who had learned their skills from acknowledged masters. 'They would have started at an early age,' said Simon. 'It was the law, for one thing: men had to learn to use a bow. But boys would see their fathers using the bow and want to have a go at it themselves anyway.'

And the awesome power of the longbow was a great leveller. 'It didn't matter whether you were a king, a duke, a knight or whatever; you could still be shot and killed at long range by a simple man of the land.'

Bowmen did not have to be particularly strong individuals. Any man of average strength, preferably one who worked with his hands for a living, was capable of becoming a lethal shot, and he didn't even have to learn any handling skills. 'There isn't really a technique to shooting a bow,' said Simon Stanley. 'Your body tends to be a bit idle in that way; it tends to find the easiest way to draw the bow, and gets used to doing it like that. All archers have different styles.'

A good medieval archer could pinpoint and hit a man at 90 metres. Aiming at a cluster of men, he could have relied on a hit from 230 metres. If there was a downside to such capability, it was that the day-to-day stresses of wielding a bow, particularly a longbow firing heavy military arrows, produced abnormal development in the bones of the back and the arms. A quarter of the skeletons from the Towton grave pit did show unusual bone changes that could have been the result of physical stress on the hands, arms and back. The question for the Bradford team was whether these changes could have been caused by pulling the longbow. Chris Knusel, the biological anthropologist, has a scientist's instinctive caution and wasn't about to jump to conclusions:

> One of the most commonly asked questions is: are these guys archers? Although I can't say they are, not hand on heart, it seems to me that pulling a very powerful bow, repeatedly, from a young age, perhaps a bow that was meant for an adult, would cause those bones to respond by building up a greater density and a greater cross-section.

To tighten his theory, Chris needed to compare the Towton bones with those of a present-day bowman. Few people fit the profile of a medieval archer, but Simon Stanley comes very close. He is in his thirties and has used the longbow since childhood. He has been shooting with really heavy bows for fourteen years. So have the years of work with the heavy longbow produced changes in Simon Stanley's body similar to those seen in the Towton soldiers? To find out, Simon agreed to get into a body scanner.

The tunnel-like machine used for the investigation employs the system known as magnetic resonance imaging (MRI). It works on the principle that the nuclei of hydrogen atoms, when subjected to a magnetic field, line up in one direction. When a radio frequency is pointed at these atoms, the alignment of their nuclei changes. As soon as the radio frequency is switched off, the nuclei realign themselves, and as they do so they emit a small electrical signal. That tiny signal is the key to MRI. The human body contains a lot of hydrogen atoms; as the internal body structures and tissues respond to short bursts of radio signals from the scanner, the resulting electrical signals translate into computer images that show accurately detailed, slice-by-slice images of the inside of the body. Because the process uses radio waves, it is much safer than X-rays or gamma rays. It is a non-invasive procedure and, though very expensive, extremely useful for detecting fluid in the brain, spinal abnormalities and the early stages of cancer.

In Simon's case, his arms were individually scanned, then the slice-by-slice pictures were viewed and evaluated by Chris Knusel and a consultant radiologist, Dr Patrick Ander. Their verdict, after meticulous comparison, was that Simon's arms had developed in exactly the same way as those of the grave warriors.

This did not prove that the more heavily developed skeletons from the pit had been archers, but it was now a more probable hypothesis. It was possible that those men had been deadly fighters who could shoot fifteen arrows a minute, the kind of warriors who had trounced and routed the best of the French armies, only to meet their end in the bleak environs of Towton.

Among the bodies was one that stood out from the rest. He was a strong-boned man in his late forties, spread eagled among his comrades but still very distinct. 'As we excavated him,' recalled Tim Sutherland, 'it was obvious that this guy was very robust. His bones were not large, but they were substantial. He just looked like a big muscly guy.'

In death he's known simply as Number 16. As on the other skeletons in the pit, the blows that ended his life were plain to see, but for the Bradford team there was another revelation: Number 16 and eleven others showed older scars, the results of massive wounds from battles long before Towton. There were signs of a demanding daily life, too. Numerous lesions known as Schmorl's nodes were found on several spinal columns; the nodes or lumps are caused by the pulpy core of the spinal discs being squeezed into the bone of the vertebra – usually a result of repeated heavy lifting. There was also evidence of a condition of the shoulder blades known as *os acromiale*; this is a condition where a bony connection at the highest point of the shoulder becomes fibrous through strain and wear. It is often associated with tearing of the rotator cuff muscles, which stabilize the shoulders. On the skulls it was relatively easy to distinguish between the wounds that caused death and the older injuries, which showed rounding of the wound edges, a sign of healing. The initial impression was that these were the bones of hard-worked men who had seen the horrors of infantry battle, yet had gone back, some of them several times.

The face of Number 16 carries the most dramatic of the healed wounds. He was examined, along with the other eleven skeletons showing old scarring, by Shannon Novak, a forensic anthropologist on second-ment to Bradford from the University of Utah. She is widely experienced in her field, and her past work has included the investigation of present-day war graves in Croatia. With Number 16 and the others, she would be evaluating the effects of violence inflicted five centuries ago.

My aim was to document the trauma in the same way I would a modern forensic case, trying to understand the number and types of wounds they had and to interpret from them some of the weapons used. And of course I wanted to look at wounds that they'd survived.

When he died, Number 16 was almost fifty years old. He would have been born at or near the time of Agincourt. His lifetime had been dominated by warfare, and at least once before Towton he had come close to dying. 'Individual 16 received a very, *very* large blade wound to the left side of the jaw,' Shannon said. 'The force was so great that it caused a secondary fracture to the chin.'

The shock alone from such an injury could have killed him, yet Number 16 survived, the wounds healed and he went back to the trade of fighting man. On the battlefield at Towton he would have been in good company, since many of the seasoned soldiers who fought on both sides in the Wars of the Roses had gained their experience in the late stages of the Hundred Years War. This veteran status existed at all ranks. They would have been men with fearful scars and ghastly tales to tell. What was remarkable was just how cleanly their war wounds had healed, and that revealed something else to the Bradford team: battle-field surgery in the fifteenth century was far more skilful and effective than had previously been believed. Shannon Novak was as surprised as any of the team, particularly by the apparent absence of infection in the earlier injuries. Deep wounds infect easily, and on a battlefield, where one blade would have been used to cut several different men, the likelihood of infection was high. Yet the deformity and destruction of bone so typical of infected war wounds was not present to any significant degree.

The accomplished surgery with which Number 16 was patched up shifts medical texts of the time into a new light. Illustrated manuals were used to pass on techniques originally acquired from the Arabs, and they show doctors practising surgery of the most ambitious kind. Until recently the books had not been taken wholly seriously. But reconstructing a man's jaw was one operation explained in the books which obviously worked. Dr Linda Paterson of Warwick University expanded on this:

> There are quite detailed instructions on how to deal with a wound to the jaw. The first stage was to put wax on the place where the bone was cut, then put a double layer of dressing over the site. Next they used a splint or a piece of shoe leather the length of the jaw, which was very carefully bandaged on to the head and sewn on to a skullcap.

The scarred and battered skull of Number 16 became the focus of intense speculation; the mystery of his identity began to stand for all that was still unknown about the Towton dead. Malin Holst said that the more they examined the skull of Number 16, the more they were astonished by it:

> We just couldn't believe what we were seeing – that somebody with such a severe injury to the jaw, and presumably to the tongue and to the soft tissues in the mouth, could have survived such a trauma and been able to function properly. I presume Number 16 would have looked quite impressively horrific to other people.

So what had Number 16 looked like? The Bradford team decided to find out. They asked forensic artist Richard Neave to make a reconstruction of his head as it would have appeared at the time of Towton.

There were problems with that kind of project. The blows that finally killed Number 16 had completely destroyed his left eye socket, his left cheekbone, part of his upper jaw, a portion of his forehead and half of his nose. Since the skull was the only reference point to guide him in the reconstruction, Richard Neave would have to make informed assumptions about the shape and proportions of the missing pieces. Even the intact facial structures presented difficulties, as Neave himself said:

> The lower jaw has been severely traumatized, probably eight to ten years prior to death, struck by a blade, horizontally across the body of the mandible. The really difficult thing is going to be how we represent that on the reconstruction, trying to ascertain his appearance with what would clearly be a very big scar across that part of the face.

The rebuilding of Number 16's face would be a long, painstaking job. Even so, Richard Neave pointed out that the technique of forensic reconstruction runs along logical and well-organized lines, so uncertainties would be kept to a minimum:

> The skull is the armature. It provides the basis on which the face and head are built. If you are doing figurative portraiture, one of the things you have to get right, to ensure that the model looks like the face of the person you're copying, is getting the proportions right: the width between the eyes, the distance between the eyes and the mouth, the size of the nose and the width and height of the face, and so on. If you have a skull, what more perfect armature could you have to work on? It already determines the exact proportions of the face.

Richard and his assistant employed basic anatomical science to develop the broad muscle groups over the surface of the copied skull, allowing the face to grow outwards. They used tables of soft-tissue measurements which help to ensure that the amount of tissue they build on to the face is consistent with known scientific standards and norms. It is not guesswork. 'The combination of measurements, statistics and basic *mechanical* anatomy allows that face to grow of its own accord. It's an exercise that can be undertaken by a number of people; it's not a magical thing.'

Muscles would be built on individually, with adjustments made where they might have been severed or otherwise damaged. The difficult part, Richard said, would be rebuilding the unknowable areas:

> While the skull will give us the proportions and the dimensions, what it can't do is to tell us exactly what the tip of the nose is like. It can't tell us the expression of the eyes, or the exact shape of a person's eyebrows, or whether they've got forehead creases either vertical or horizontal. In this instance, we're going to have the right proportions. His face is slightly twisted; it's asymmetrical. He's going to have his scar; it'll be in the right place, the right shape, right size, which will give an indication of how he might have looked. Basically it's a mechanical exercise.

The way in which Number 16's scars had healed provides a clue to his earlier life. The sophistication of the surgery that saved him suggests he was connected to a noble household. Dr Linda Paterson expanded on this:

> On the whole, the people who would have received medical treatment would have been rich people. On the other hand,

I think it's clear that surgeons were not simply treating knights. Some instructions in the medical books are prefaced with the words, 'If a sergeant goes into battle poorly armed and without an iron hat, then he may well suffer from this kind of wound'. What this suggests to me is that people who were employing surgeons in their armies were interested in the survival of their professional warriors.

There were few professional soldiers in the armies of that time. Most fighting men on the battlefields had no choice but to be there. A number of noblemen did have a retinue of paid fighting men, singled out from an early age, thoroughly trained and dressed in their masters' livery. Was Number 16 a member of an elite corps? Biological anthropologist Chris Knusel believed it was likely:

I can see him in my mind, and I think he must have been a livery soldier. He appears to have trained from a very young age, before he was physiologically mature, and what I mean by that is that some time prior to the age of, say, fourteen or fifteen he would already have been training. In addition to that, he's a very broad individual, which may suggest either he's that way because of this intensive training or he was *selected* because he's a broad individual.

Whether they were retainers or not, Number 16 and the other scarred individuals from the pit were experienced warriors. But even for them, Towton must have been a fresh horror. 'So great was the slaughter of men,' wrote Edward Hall, 'that the very carcasses hindered them that fought.'

The figure of 28,000 dead, counted by the heralds, began to circulate within a matter of weeks. Today, this total raises disbelief in some people, such as Matthew Bennett of the Royal Military Academy:

> I think 28,000 dead is a totally implausible number. If you accept that, then it's rather like accepting that more men died at Towton than did in the disastrous first day of the Somme on 1 July 1916, when they actually advanced against machine guns in open fields.

Andrew Boardman takes a less sceptical view:

> A chronicler of the period, the Abbot of St Albans, said there were 20,000 Lancastrians killed. Elsewhere there are letters of the period that give a total figure of 28,000. Another chronicler decided there were 33,000 killed. Everybody at that time seemed to have a different number.

The figure that appears to have most corroboration, however, is 28,000. Three letters written soon after the battle quote that figure, all three seemingly from independent and well-informed sources. George Neville reports in his chronicles that his brother, the Earl of Warwick, who actually fought in the battle, told him that 28,000 men died. 'You can safely say that it was a very, very big battle by medieval standards,' Andrew said, 'but specific figures are hard to nail down. It's really a case of which set of chronicles you believe, and bear in mind what seems a believable figure for casualties. But 28,000 is the figure quoted with most authority.'

The Bradford team were keen that the grave pit should yield evidence of the nature of the killing at Towton. Shannon Novak, more familiar with gunshots than sword cuts, began working out ways to identify the weapons that produced the wounding on the skeletons. One method she used was to take a dry block of rigid foam, used in the preparation of flower arrangements, and to insert into it the tips of weapons of the various kinds that were used at the Battle of Towton. When the weapons were pulled out of the foam, they left behind perfectly profiled holes. These profiles were then compared with the wound shapes visible on the skeletons. As the catalogue of injuries and their probable causes grew, Shannon noted that the most common cause of death had been blade wounds from sword, dagger or battleaxe. Other stabbing wounds came from the spike of a pole-axe or a horseman's hammer, the blows being delivered while the victims apparently lay on the ground. Shannon found only one arrow wound.

So Number 16 and his companions were attacked and killed at close quarters. Almost without exception they died from blows directly to the head, but over and above that fact the wound patterns showed something curious: it appeared that the men's heads had been completely unprotected, yet no soldier would have deliberately left off his helmet. To do so would have been suicidal. On the evidence as it stood, it could be surmised that these men had been singled out for punishment. By careful study of the wounds, Chris Knusel could determine that the victims had first been dealt single, savage blows to the head, serious enough to kill them, and then, incredibly, they had been hit several more times on the head and face.

'My own feeling is that some of these individuals may have still been living when they received the second, tertiary and subsequent blows.' It was, Chris said, as if the first blow was designed to render the men less able to defend themselves against what followed. 'Essentially, it's a massacre.'

The notion of a massacre upsets conventional ideas about the importance of chivalry in medieval times. Battles, it has been generally assumed, were conducted according to a code of honour. If that were the case, the code was conspicuously absent from Towton.

Originally, the word 'chivalry' referred to the knightly class of feudal times. The accepted sense in the Middle Ages was 'knights', or 'fully armed and mounted fighting men'. In time the meaning evolved to become 'the honour and gallantry expected of knights'.

For a time the lines of the concept hardened. The Court of Chivalry was established in the fourteenth century by Edward III; the Earl Marshal of England and the Lord High Constable sat as joint judges. They had the power of summary jurisdiction in all cases concerning offences by knights. When the Earl Marshal alone took charge of the court, it became strictly a court of honour, making decisions on precedence and the suitability and permissibility of certain coats of arms. No case came before that court from 1737 to 1954. In 1954 the court convened, with the Earl Marshal presiding, to consider a petition from Manchester City Corporation, who alleged the improper use of the city's coat of arms by the Manchester Palace of Varieties.

The importance of chivalry in the sense of 'honour and gallantry expected of knights' was reinforced by the Crusades, which led to the creation of the earliest orders of chivalry: the Order of the Hospital of St John of Jerusalem (Hospitallers) and the Order of the Poor Knights of Christ and of the Temple of Solomon (Templars). These orders were nominally committed to the service of pilgrims to the Holy Land. In the fourteenth and fifteenth centuries, however, the standards and exemplars of chivalry became connected increasingly with aristocratic display and public ceremony, rather than service in the field.

The notion of the courtly knights displaying high-bred courtesy as a matter of habit, and rescuing damsels whenever necessary, is a comforting myth. So, it seems, is the idea of a fifteenth-century knight granting mercy to a vanquished adversary. 'It was an aristocratic idea which only extended to other knights,' said Dr Linda Paterson. 'I think they had no compunction at all about mistreating anyone who was not a knight.'

It was certainly true that the ruling orders did not consider a common soldier's life to have any significant value. By the end of the fourteenth century, feudalism had ceased to be a social and political force in England, but it had left its marks. Feudal society was a system of privileges and obligations based on land tenure and on relationships in which land was held 'in fief' or 'in feudal benefice' by vassals from lords – a vassal defined as 'a tenant in fee'. The vassals owed rents and services in return for land and, moreover, were bound to their lords by an obligation of loyalty. By the time of the Battle of Towton the principles of that system still more or less prevailed, except that the lords by then held more power than previously. On the battlefield the mistreatment of common soldiery was no worse to a knight, or any other nobleman, than whipping a dog.

What the mistreatment might have involved was becoming apparent in the laboratory. Some of the wounds inflicted on the Towton men near the time of their death were disturbingly unusual. Skulls showed repeated shallow cuts to the ears, scalp and face. To Chris Knusel they raised an odious possibility:

> We have at least one individual that seems to have had his nose targeted. Also, there are some scratches above the left ear on one individual, a series of parallel scratches. They're incised, so it's not chopping; it's a kind of cutting, which may suggest that an ear or a part of the ear and the scalp were removed. Which may suggest that we're dealing with a case of mutilation.

For a time, suspicions about mistreatment and mutilation appeared to be supported by the position in the grave of another skeleton, Number 24. When the team first uncovered his remains, they had found both arms twisted behind him, which appeared to present an inescapable conclusion. 'We thought he might have been a prisoner with his arms tied behind his back,' said Malin Holst. 'His legs were touching at the knees, which was also unusual. So we thought this might turn out to be a very important skeleton in the analysis.'

Tim Sutherland said different notions ran through his mind when he looked at Number 24: 'One would assume that he would have been captured, or somebody would have had to tie his arms behind his back. And there was the idea that this individual may have been tortured and may have really suffered before he died of his injuries.'

A distressing picture was emerging from the fragmentary evidence: men lined up by the grave pit, stripped, mutilated and executed. The scenario has been common enough in conflicts in our own times, but it clashes with our ingrained – if unreliable – sentiments about chivalry. This veteran soldier, Number 24, had fought in a number of battles, but was it likely that his last one ended with his being captured and put to death?

The archaeologists' knowledge of the men from Towton was accumulating. They knew that the soldiers in the grave had been killed by multiple blows to the head; some of them had been mutilated at the point of death, and there were suspicions of one or more executions. They had even speculated that since one man's hands appeared to have been tied, perhaps all the soldiers had been under restraint at the time of their death. However, Shannon Novak's work on the wounds was beginning to suggest that Number 16, Number 24 and the others might have died in unrestrained circumstances. She made the point that at some stage these men had their arms and hands free to defend themselves:

Most of the wounds that occur in the bodies are on the arms and the hands, and these are classic defence wounds. For example, in homicide with stabbings, you'll often see individuals with extensive cuts to their hands, down to the bone, because they'll grab the blade. What we see at Towton are reminiscent of defence wounds, a fact which says to me that their hands weren't bound.

Independently, Tim Sutherland was arriving at the same conclusion. During the original excavation, Number 24 appeared to be lying with his arms behind him, and the assumption was that his hands had been tied in that position. But at the bottom of the grave pit a single severed arm was found, quite separate from any body. At first, the archaeologists thought it must be an amputation. However, when Tim Sutherland went back to the laboratory and carefully separated his 3-D images of the grave, he found that the spare arm wasn't spare at all – it belonged to Number 24. 'With the computer work we had analysed each individual skeleton in an attempt to match the spare arm with one of the bodies. What actually happened was that Number 24 had been superimposed exactly over the spare arm.'

In the small flurry of the original dig, Number 24 had been allocated the arm of a neighbouring skeleton, which gave the impression that he had both arms behind him. The 3-D image now revealed that his arms could not have been tied. So there was no reason, after all, to believe that the grave-pit warriors had died helpless victims.

In the meantime, as Number 16 was being moulded back to a semblance of life by Richard Neave, the question of how he died still exercised the Bradford team. Their work was helped greatly by Simon Richardson, who added an extra perspective to their work – metal detection. Few people have a better overview of the Battle of Towton than Simon, who has been searching the battlefield for sixteen years.

> I do imagine what it would have been like, what the people would have been like. I think about the injuries the men would have received and probably the screams, the men crying. It must have been pretty horrendous. When I started out, I expected to find battleaxes and swords, breastplates and helmets, but it turned out quite different from that.

Simon's discoveries on the battlefield have been small but revealing in their personal detail: there has been a signet ring, a buckle from a harness or armour, the tip of a scabbard, a broken spur. These are the fallout from hand-to-hand fighting, or items lost in flight or in death. 'It feels quite personal when I find the artefacts. I think of the last person to wear something – did they actually die, or was it pulled off and they managed to escape?'

Simon plots the position of every item he discovers and shares his data with the archaeologists, helping to build up a picture of the ebb and flow of the battle. His 300 finds confirm that the main battle did take place where tradition says it did. Towton Hall, where the skeletons were found, is a kilometre and a half away from the battlefield. There is speculation over how the men came to be there. Were they taken to the hall as prisoners, or carried there dead, or were they killed in the final phase of the battle? The chronicles say that the worst slaughter at Towton came in the rout as the Lancastrians ran from the battlefield. The valley that had protected their flank became their killing ground.

Andrew Boardman, author and authority on the battle, explained that the worst possible thing to do in any battle is for soldiers to turn their backs on the enemy:

> My personal opinion is those men in the grave were caught in the rout. The injuries they sustained have the appearance of attacks that were made when they were down on the ground. Dagger wounds to the backs of the heads: repeated injuries, not something you'd probably find if you were in a battle, actually caught up in the fighting. If you hit a man and he went down, then that would be enough because you would be looking for someone else to come at you from a different angle. The injuries here were multiple, and there are even signs of mutilation; all of that points to a rout rather than a battle.

Using forensic techniques that she has employed on murder investigations, Shannon Novak began to sequence the men's wounds. The way in which the lines of fracture connect on the skulls indicates the order of the blows, and that order suggests that some men could have been running away from whoever killed them.

Shannon demonstrated her technique of ascribing a sequence to multiple injuries. The skull she used had a massive gash transversely across the back. There was also a very large blade wound to the face. 'The facial blade cut runs from the corner of the left eye, down underneath the nose, through the palate and into the root of a tooth.'

Because of the sheer force of the blow, the facial wound created a fracture that travelled up along the front of the skull; then the crack stops where it meets another fracture which runs side to side across the top of the skull. Because the frontal fracture stops at that point, it tells Shannon that the side-to-side fracture was already in place when the soldier received the blade wound to the face. 'The energy release from the facial blow started to follow the fracture that already existed. So we know that first of all this man received a large, probably mortal wound to the back of the head. While he was presumably down, a blade was drawn through his face.'

What she held in her hands, Shannon added, was the evidence of war. 'These are the men that were there and didn't make it out, and this is what weapons were created for, to be efficient killing tools.'

Though the figures may be disputed, it is certain that very many men died at the Battle of Towton. Those who didn't die that day have a monument, but the ones who are certainly not forgotten are the thirty-seven men from the pit near Towton Hall, as the University of Bradford team work on to learn more about them. As Malin Holst said:

> I do feel as if I know them very well. I feel that some are particularly close to me, and I feel particularly for what some of them must have undergone. And it's an incredible thought that most of the people who fought and died on the battlefield or in the surrounding area are still there.

Much about the battle remains a mystery, but the discovery of the skeletons in the shallow grave, which arguably raise more questions than they answer, has given science the opportunity to uncover a little more of a misunderstood past. The answers to the remaining questions can only be found, if at all, from discoveries at the battlefield. Of the many thousands of bodies buried there, no more have turned up, so the archaeologists still rely on the thirty-seven skeletons from the pit to enlarge on the patchy and decidedly grim story that has emerged.

For young Edward IV of the House of York the Battle of Towton was a glorious, resounding triumph, and he returned to London to be crowned the one true king. But the Wars of the Roses did not end at Towton. They dragged on for another twenty-four years, costing thousands more lives. Then Henry Tudor (later Henry VII), the last hope of the Lancastrians, killed the man who was then king, Richard III, at Bosworth Field in 1485. The following year Henry married Edward IV's daughter, Elizabeth of York, thus uniting the Yorkist and Lancastrian claims. Henry's defeat of a Yorkist uprising in support of the pretender Lambert Simnel on 16 June 1487 provided the date preferred by some historians over the traditional 1485 for the ending of the wars.

For one of the Towton dead, Number 16, Richard Neave's reconstruction is an impressive memorial. 'I think now that he's got flesh on his face you can really imagine him as a person,' said Malin Holst. 'He's a live character who actually existed and was present in the battle. He certainly looks mature and experienced. It would have been hard to face him in a battle situation; he would have been scary.'

Neave's model puts an impressively human countenance on the old campaigner, showing him to be a disfigured man with strong features, and the kind of gaze that sees beyond appearances. He has the determined look of an individual stripped of all illusion, a soldier who knew that you made your own luck on the field of battle.

2

CANYON CANNIBALS

IN THE REGION OF THE American South-West, where the boundaries of Arizona, New Mexico and Colorado intersect, the Anasazi culture spread and flourished for more than a thousand years. Until recently the sparse history that survived these early native Americans told us that they were an industrious and progressive people whose civilization lasted from around AD 100 to some time in the twelfth century. They were given the name Anasazi – 'the Ancient Ones' — by the Navajo, who migrated to the region at the end of the thirteenth century. At that time a few Anasazi remained in the area, living in tiny hill settlements, surviving by hunting and limited crop-farming. However, from the impressive surroundings it was clear to the Navajo that these people had once been part of a substantial and powerful culture.

Throughout the region the Navajo found meticulously constructed villages, elegantly planned towns and even cities, all of them abandoned. In some cases dwellings and whole villages had been built in sheltered recesses in the faces of cliffs, and elsewhere large, free-standing, multi-apartment structures stood along canyons or mesa walls. Many houses had two, three or even four storeys, built in stepped-back style to let the roofs of the lower rooms serve as balconies for the ones above. These places were not put together from wood and earth like the adobe houses elsewhere in the region; they were built from hundreds of thousands of tonnes of stone blocks, neatly veneered with slabs of sandstone. Even though the Anasazi had no wheeled transport or pack animals, they managed to haul massive timbers of western yellow pine many kilometres from faraway forests to be used for roofing. Grand open plazas were built in the centre of the towns, and there were chambers called kivas, built wholly or partly underground, used by the males of the Anasazi for religious rites.

The Navajo also discovered that the Anasazi had been basketweavers, potters and decorative painters. Specimens of their multiple talents were to be found in profusion. They wove blankets from rabbit fur, fashioned wind chimes from copper and made trinkets inlaid with turquoise, mica and shell. The Navajo did not disturb any of the artefacts they found, fearing that some magical taint might adhere to stolen objects, especially any taken from that eerily deserted locale.

Inevitably, archaeologists and historians looked on the Anasazi as a thoroughly admirable people. The traces of their existence they left showed their industrious and democratic way of life to be near-Utopian. Here was a model society if ever there was one: they cultivated maize; they developed an understanding of the constellations and kept astronomical records; they created fine architecture supported by efficient engineering and urban planning; their pottery was beautifully fashioned and decorated with fine art.

But everything stopped around AD 1200. The society's structure collapsed, and the Anasazi disappeared. All that remains of them are the ruins of their buildings, and their bones. Today, new forensic findings have begun to cast this ancient, supposedly peace-loving people in a very different light. Our view of the Anasazi is being turned upside down, and unearthing the facts has been the lifelong obsession of one man, Professor Christy Turner. He has spent the last thirty years studying the ancient peoples of the South-West, investigating the skeletal remains of men, women and children. He explained that scientific detachment had its limits: it was not easy to stay dispassionate when examining the remains of a child. As he spoke, he held up the upper frontal part of a child's skull to demonstrate his point.

> If we look at it very closely, we can begin to see things about the child. We can tell from the kinds of dental wear, and the kinds of dental damage, that the child had been relatively healthy up to a certain point. But this episode stopped the child's life. Notice that the nose is broken, the blown-out sockets of the teeth ... We think this kind of damage results from being hit in the face with a stone. But we cannot tell if the child was alive or if it was dead at the time this happened.

Once a forensic consultant for the police, now a professor at Arizona State University, Turner has devoted his entire career to investigating a unique brand of violence. He believes that the ancient peoples of the South-West were much more brutal than was historically accepted.

> The Anasazi have been portrayed as peaceful, happy farmers with no problems. But you will see the evidence of violence, of warfare, almost every place you look. Now, people don't seem to have any problem with violence. You can attack a town, kill 800 people, nobody gets too excited. But people have a big problem watching our evidence say that someone was being eaten ...

Cannibalism. Clinical manuals and volumes on abnormal psychology call it anthropophagy, the eating of human flesh by humans. The word 'cannibal' was originally one of the forms of the ethnic name Carib or Caribes, a fierce nation of the West Indies, recorded to have been man-eaters, or *anthropophagi,* and from whom the name was taken as a term of description.

Cannibalism was once widespread and is rooted in the earliest years of human history. It has been practised by the peoples of most continents, and although many of the early descriptions were probably exaggerated or simply wrong, the practice certainly went on into modern times in parts of West and Central Africa, Fiji, New Guinea, Australia, among the Maoris of New Zealand, in parts of Polynesia, Sumatra and among several of the tribes of North and South America.

Some cultures have regarded human flesh an acceptable form of food. Maoris, if they were on the winning side in a battle, were often noted to cut up the bodies of their dead enemies and devour them. Before the Dutch brought them fully under control, the Batak of Sumatra sold human flesh in their markets.

In other times and circumstances the eating of particular cuts or specific organs was a ritual way of acquiring certain qualities of the person being eaten. Cannibalism in Africa was often related to sorcery; head-hunters and other predatory groups ate pieces of the bodies of dead enemies as a way of absorbing their adversaries' vitality and diminishing their capacity for revenge.

In 1896 the German anthropologist R. S. Steinmetz coined the word 'endocannibalism' to label the practice of 'eating parents and relatives', and it is known that Aborigines in Australia carried out the same practice as an act of respect.

There have been periods when ritual pseudo-cannibalism has formed a part of the drama of secret societies. In cannibalistic ceremonies of the Kwakiutl Indians on the north-west coast of America, for instance, a novice seemingly possessed by the cannibal spirit would eat the flesh of a dead body, or bite a piece from the arm or leg of a living person, before he was calmed and brought back to a psychologically normal state. These dramas, however, were staged purely for their alarming effect on the audience – the Kwakiutl and neighbouring tribes detested the eating of human flesh.

In recent times Dr Daniel Carleton Gajdusek, an American physician and medical researcher, became co-recipient of the 1976 Nobel Prize for Physiology or Medicine for his work in implicating slow-acting viruses as the cause of certain degenerative neurological disorders. Gajdusek discovered a unique central nervous system disorder and provided the first medical description of it ever published; it was a disease that occurred only among the Fore people of New Guinea and was known to them as 'kuru' (trembling). Gajdusek lived for a while among the Fore and studied their culture. He also performed autopsies on kuru victims and finally came to the conclusion that the disease was transmitted by the ritualistic eating of the brains of deceased relatives, which was a funerary custom of the Fore.

Gajdusek's name came to public attention again three years after his Nobel award when a debate arose – and still rumbles on – over the claim made by William Arens in his book *The Man-Eating Myth* that cannibalism has never actually happened.

Arens, an anthropologist, wrote that historians and ethnographers had failed to present any reliable evidence or useful eyewitness accounts of anthropophagy. Arens pointed out that Dr Gajdusek, who had been uniquely placed to be a witness, hadn't seen it either. Most descriptions of cannibalism were in European books and learned papers, ascribing savage acts to the inhabitants of far-flung places – acts that, Arens insisted, no one can put hand on heart and say he or she has witnessed. To the annoyance of many well-informed and balanced opponents of Arens' point of view, no dependable witnesses have yet come forward.

Fuelling the debate are the suspect chronicling tactics of the sixteenth-century Spaniards, whose own treatment of Jews and Muslims had exceeded even medieval standards of atrocity. When they came upon the similarly murderous peoples of Central and South America, they claimed to be appalled, and proceeded to do more than just chronicle the awful practices of Aztecs and Chibchas. The Spaniards actually blamed them for the invention of cannibalism. In the eighteenth and nineteenth centuries any part of the southern hemisphere explored by Europeans produced stories of people devouring human flesh, stories that, detractors insist, were no more than distorted reports of funeral customs in which flesh, bones, hair or even eyes were mixed with food in an effort to transmit some of the qualities of the deceased to those who had survived them.

Until recently an air of professional distaste, amounting in some cases to abhorrence, has typified the scientific community's attitude to research centring on cannibalism. It was not an area where many would venture. Christy Turner, on the other hand, has had no qualms about following a line of research wherever it would lead. He admits, however, that his investigation of the Anasazi has at times caused him personal distress:

> If you infer what happened and you follow the inferences and their logical tracks, you come to a very, very emotional set of events. The history indicates that people are screaming. The women are begging not to be killed; the men who try to help them get mutilated. They

mutilate the people while they are alive; they're cutting their arms off while they're alive … If you let yourself see these things, it becomes very difficult to be objective about what you're dealing with.

In 1969, while he was still a young professor, Turner presented a controversial paper that described his evidential findings of cannibalism in the American South-West. The paper was roundly rejected, but Turner was resolutely committed to his research. He persevered. Over the following three decades, along with his late wife Jacqueline, he amassed formidable evidence of cannibalistic practices. These findings, which he presents – and vigorously defends – in the classroom and in his publications, are only now changing our understanding of Anasazi society.

To say that Turner has his detractors would be to understate the case quite seriously. The findings of his research have led to his being attacked and ridiculed. Among his most vociferous opponents are Native American tribes like the Zuni, the Hopi and their clans, who claim they are descendants of the Anasazi. They find Turner's claims shockingly inaccurate.

'First of all, on the issue of violence and cannibalism,' said Leigh Kuwanwisiwma of the Cultural Preservation Office of the Hopi tribe, 'we do have some memory of different types of violent behaviour inflicted on Hopi people. We do not have any traditions about any of the sixty or so clans that we know once existed inflicting any kind of behaviour so extreme against any other Hopi clan.'

But Turner believes he has identified clear and convincing evidence of cannibalism. The findings come from Chaco Canyon in north-west New Mexico, established as a national monument in 1907. It occupies an area of 88 square kilometres and consists of a canyon dissected by the Chaco and Gallo washes, which are deep tracts or fissures caused by the river's overflow. The ruined sites of thirteen major pre-Columbian Indian communities and over three hundred smaller archaeological sites are located in the canyon. Pueblo Bonito, dating from the tenth century, is the largest and most completely excavated building in the canyon; it had an estimated eight hundred rooms and thirty-two kivas. The excavations mainly demonstrate that the people of Chaco Canyon excelled in tool-making, weaving, pottery, farming and masonry. But Turner's interest has lain in other, less apparent areas of tribal history. Time and again he has gone back to examine the bones discovered in and around this canyon by early archaeologists – long-neglected collections stacked in museums across America.

When the first archaeologists visited Chaco in the late nineteenth century, they found an abundance of bone fragments among the stones. Most ancient burial sites are orderly in their arrangement of skeletons, demonstrating a universal reverence for the dead. But in the South-West, some Anasazi sites were different. Bones were found in a distorted condition, or crushed and scattered. None of the early archaeologists knew precisely what it all signified, although a few had their suspicions. Trader, guide and pioneering archaeologist Richard Wetherill led the first major expedition into Chaco Canyon in the 1890s. The field director of those excavations wrote:

> Some of our workmen cleaned out a number of rooms, and in one of these a great many human bones were found. Some of these, including portions of the skull, were charred, and the majority of the long bones had been cracked open. It would therefore seem that these Pueblo Indians, either through stress of hunger or for religious reasons, had occasionally resorted to the eating of human flesh.

Many of Wetherill's findings were widely disputed, then later dismissed or ignored. Wetherill himself was murdered in 1910. The story goes that on the evening of 22 June he and a cowboy called Bill Finn were driving a few cattle along a bend in Chaco Canyon, just short of a kilometre below Pueblo Bonito. They reached a point where a wagon trail cuts up through scattered rock to the high mesa; a group of five or six Navajo were standing there when Wetherill and Finn came by. At Rincon del Camino, the place where Wetherill died, the road turned to cross the shallow end of a trough among rocks and prickly, waist-high greasewood vegetation. It is said the coloration is such that a person's eyes, adjusting from the brightness of a low sun to the smoky blue shadows, could easily take a motionless man or horse for a feature of the landscape. For these reasons, and because the cattle were probably raising a cloud of dust, Wetherill and the cowboy saw no signs of danger before it was too late.

In the greasewood bordering the trough, a Navajo standing by his horse raised his rifle, a .33-calibre Winchester, and fired two shots. The first whistled past Bill Finn's head; the second went through Richard Wetherill's right hand and into his chest. It killed him at once. The Navajo walked the short distance to where the body had fallen and crouched down over it. 'Are you sick, Anasazi?' he asked. When there was no response, he pointed his rifle downwards. The third shot destroyed the right side of Wetherill's head.

Finn escaped to the safety of the Wetherill ranch. Whatever the reason for Wetherill's murder, it was never thought to have had anything to do with his work. The murderer probably had no idea who he was.

Professor Turner regards Wetherill and his colleagues as trailblazers. 'They have identified cannibalism,' he said. 'They have identified violence. They did not have an explanation, but they got it right, they got it right. What bothers me is: why is my profession ignoring what these people did?'

Retracing the footsteps of Wetherill and the archaeologists who followed, Turner was able to confirm that what they had found among these hills was not the typical archaeological detritus of any graveyard. In at least one in every fifty cases, the trail led to murder. The bodies had been dismembered and the bones smashed to fragments. The ancient remains reminded Turner of the way in which the early hunters handled the game they ate.

In conducting his long research into the Anasazi, one of the first things Turner tried to do was to get inside their minds. A major part of the process was to perform many of the typical manual chores of the Anasazi menfolk; in pursuing the mystery of the smashed bones, he turned his hand to butchering meat, demonstrating in the process how difficult it can be.

'This stuff is so tough,' he said, chopping at a ribbed section of beef with a sharpened stone. 'It won't come apart.' He resorted to putting the bony meat on the ground and battering it with a rock. 'Look at all these fragments. Look at all these little, tiny pieces that have come from my hitting this bone.' Mangled meat and chipped particles of bone stuck to his fingers. 'This is what goes into the pot. This is meat processing. We're talking about processing of people for the same reason they're processing animals. This is how it's done.'

To turn a human into meat is an act so reviled that the charge has outraged many Native Americans. Turner's claims strike them as no less than historical slander. In the face of doubt, rejection and condemnation from Native Americans and scientists alike, Turner set himself the highest standards of procedure. He developed a series of forensic indicators that would have to be present before he could claim that human remains had been cut, cooked and eaten. There are now a minimum of six criteria that have to be present before a conclusion of cannibalism may be drawn:

• Cuts and other tool marks on the bones. (Probable cause: dismemberment and stripping of the flesh.)

• Bones broken open. (Probable cause: removal of marrow.)

• 'Anvil' abrasions. (Probable cause: bone was placed on an anvil stone and smashed with a hammer stone.)

• Indications of burning, especially on back or top of skull. (Probable cause: head was placed on fire in order to cook the brain.)

• Absence of vertebrae and other bones with spongy components in their structure. (Probable cause: complete conversion of these fat-bearing bones to an edible mass by pounding or grinding or removal of the bones for boiling to extract the fatty elements.)

Tim D. White, a distinguished palaeoanthropologist, contributed the sixth criterion that Turner subsequently tested and accepted. It is the texture-transforming effect on the ends of bones described as 'pot polish'.

White's curiosity about cannibalism was first raised when he saw scratches on a fossilized African skull and thought they might have been caused by a sharp instrument used to remove the flesh. In 1985 he was loaned the skeletal remains of thirty Anasazi from an excavation site at Mancos Canyon in Colorado. Following a five-year study of the bones, White was able to announce that he had found all of Turner's criteria for determining cannibalism. At about that time, White observed a faint shine on the broken ends of several of the Colorado bones; this, he surmised, could have been caused by the bones being boiled in ceramic vessels. The Anasazi's cooking pots had a rough interior, which could have had an abrasive effect on bones as they were stirred. Bones that were too long to fit into the typical cooking vessels showed no polishing on the ends.

White tested his theory with deer bones, breaking them and putting them in a clay pot with water. He heated the water and kept it simmering for three hours, giving the bones an occasional stir. The extraction process certainly worked: fat rose in a dense ring and clung to the sides of the pot, where White easily scraped it off with a bone fragment. Later, examining the cooked deer bones under magnification, White found they had the same shine on the ends as the bones from Mancos Canyon. Furthermore, the scratches on the piece of bone he used to scrape the fat out of the pot were a match for those he had seen on a bone fragment among the Mancos skeletons. Professor Turner later carried out the same experiment using the bones of cattle and chickens. He obtained results identical to those produced by Tim White.

Turner's checklist of criteria became the foundation of a new branch of science, human taphonomy. The basic science of taphonomy involves the study of the processes by which the remains of animals and plants become preserved as fossils; human taphonomy seeks to study this process in the light of possible manipulation and altering of human remains close to the time of death.

Again using skull fragments, Turner demonstrated the kind of investigative work that has backed up his controversial conclusions:

> First off, the parts of the assemblage that we can identify with certainty are human head parts that have burning on the backs of the heads or on the tops of the heads but never on the face. So, the head has been placed on a fire for a length of time that caused the charring and the burning and the damage on the outside, but no damage on the inside. The skull was intact; the brain was still inside. In short, it was being roasted, prepared for a meal.

The demonstration was unequivocal, showing skull bones clearly damaged and charred on one side but unflawed by anything but time on the other. Turner continued his explanation:

> After the roasting, the heads were broken open to expose the brain. The procedure was to take the head, place it on an anvil stone, take a hammer stone and hit it hard, causing the skull to crack open. The cracking resulted in the skull breaking into a series of pieces, and from the bones we found we know the fracturing occurred at or around the time of death, because the breaks are very, very sharp.

Fractures in living bone – or bone of a human recently deceased – have a cleanly defined edge, quite different from the desiccated, stone-like edges found in bone that has undergone lengthy time-change and has lost the twenty-five per cent of organic material found in fresh bone.

The extraction of the cooked brain left another clear sign of cannibalism – anvil abrasion, a distinctive series of scrape marks that occur as a bone is smashed between stones. 'Those are particularly important,' said Turner, 'because you cannot get anvil abrasions on a bone that is heavily covered with muscle tissue. You must first cut the tissue off.'

Turner also discovered a pattern of tiny V-shaped grooves etched in the suspect skull bones. These were caused neither from erosion over time nor from the teeth marks of carnivores and scavengers, such as biting coyotes or gnawing rodents. They were sharp, parallel cuts, the marks of stone tools slicing away flesh and muscle and cutting swiftly to the bone.

The Anasazi were adept at the manufacture and use of stone tools. During the long Palaeolithic Period, three main types of tools appeared, with significant variations developing within each type. Refinements of these were found at Chaco. The types are known as 'core', 'flake' and 'blade'. Core tools are the biggest; the earliest ones were made by working on a fist-sized chunk of rock – core – with a similar-sized rock – hammer stone – and chipping off large flakes on one side to produce a sharp, jagged crest. Later, thinner core tools were developed which were sharper and more versatile.

Flake tools grew from a technique that developed more than two million years later. The idea was to use a more oblique angle of contact between hammer stone and core, a technique that provided much more control over the chipping process and yielded thinner-edged, sharper flakes. The flakes were kept and the core was discarded. The fully developed flake tool was therefore a purpose-made implement and not a by-product of some other procedure.

The third type, blade tools, were long shards of rock with fine, keen edges, making them versatile general-purpose cutting instruments. Alternatively, blade tools could be used as stock material for making numbers of other, smaller tools.

For the past decade Bruce Bradley, an archaeologist, has investigated the use of precisely these kinds of prehistoric implements. Using flake tools that he manufactured himself, broken from the same kind of rock the Anasazi would have used, he took Turner's fieldwork to another level. His aim, in a series of forensic experiments, was to discover the way in which the ancient Anasazi hunters would have used these tools to carve meat from bone, and to see what kind of evidence his efforts would leave on the bones. A sheep bought from a butcher's shop provided a real-world test for Turner's theories.

'Tendons are the tough things,' Bradley said as he struggled to separate meat from hide and skeleton. 'Meat is easy to cut, but the tendons are tough, and you've got a lot of them attaching muscle to the ends of the bone.'

Tendon is the connective tissue that binds muscle to other body parts and transmits the contracting muscles' mechanical force to the bones. Connected to muscle at one end and bone at the other, a tendon is made of tightly packed collagen fibres with spindle-shaped cells called fibroblasts scattered among them. This makes for an extremely strong material – it has to be, to withstand the fierce stresses created by ordinary body movement. Sometimes tendon is nearly impossible to cut because of its density and because at various points in the body the tendons have elements of bone embedded in them. Ligament, the tissue that supports the internal organs and aligns the bones at the joints, is almost identical in composition to tendon and can be every bit as hard to cut.

'I'm going to have to change tools,' Bradley said, slicing his way through yet another length of tendon. 'This one's making me bleed too much.' He held up his hands. 'Most of the blood's mine.' As he strove to reduce the sheep to its edible parts, Bradley proved that dismantling an animal is not easy, and the effort definitely leaves marks. The comparable difficulty of dismembering a human body was clear.

He cut free a front leg and held it up. 'I'm trying to disarticulate it,' he said, and began bending and twisting the leg at the joint, making it crack. 'I've got to flex it so that I can get right inside the joint. I can't just cut it apart where those tendons go between the bones. I'll end up wrenching it to get at the tendons, then cutting some more. It's not nice and clean like working with a metal saw.'

When he was through, it remained to be seen if all this manipulation and cutting would leave the kind of signs Professor Turner's criteria called for. And it did. When the processing of the carcass was complete, the cutting marks on the bones did not merely resemble those found on the Anasazi bones, they were a clear match. Even their location and distribution were the same – in groups near the ends of the bones, where tendons had held tightly to the muscle.

Besides the cut marks, Bradley produced further evidence to show that Turner's theories were firmly bedded in fact. He demonstrated with the thick upper bone from one of the sheep's legs. 'I've taken the bone out and detached it, and I want to get at the marrow.'

Marrow is as nutritious as brain. In humans and animals, the yellow marrow of the long bones serves as a storehouse for fat. To people living in Chaco Canyon during the first and the early second millennium, this nutritious material was perhaps the single most important source of fat they could ever find.

'I need to clean off the meat that's sticking to the bone itself,' said Bradley, 'because if I try to smash it without doing that, the meat is going to cushion the blow and it won't work.' He scraped the bone with a stone flake, which, he explained, would not only get rid of the meat fragments but would also strip away the periosteum, a fibrous tissue that encases bones, acting as a nerve-carrying layer and a provider of osteoblasts, which are bone-producing cells.

When Bradley had thoroughly cleaned the long bone, there were clearly visible scrape marks the same as those on Anasazi bone fragments. 'Now we put it on a flat stone and smash it with another stone.'

The bone shattered under the impact of the stone, and a smooth pinkish-yellow column of marrow was revealed. Examining the fragments later, Professor Turner explained something else that was significant. 'The length of these fragments is the same in humans as it is in game animals. They were breaking the bones up even to the same length.'

And that was the length of bone that would fit into Anasazi cooking pots. The pots themselves created further, by now predictable evidence of cannibalism; as the stew was cooked and stirred, the vessels' rough interior imparted a unique trace on the ends of the bones – pot polish.

So the Anasazi bones showed the clear markings of cannibalism, but there was one more clue to be found in what was *missing:* significant skeletal bones. In the collections of bones that showed signs of cannibalism, no vertebrae were present. 'It means the vertebrae have been destroyed,' Turner said. 'And we think this was caused by nothing more than people smashing the vertebrae to extract the marrow that's present in them as well as in the long bones like the femur, arms and so forth.'

The summary of findings was now persuasive:

> We have the breakage. We have the cutting. We have the burning. We have anvil abrasions. We have the polishing. And we add this sixth character, the missing vertebrae. And that's our goal, to make the test for cannibalism very, very severe so that we don't have false cases of cannibalism being interpreted or being proposed. Bottom line: those Anasazi were processed the same way as game animals.

Turner has asked why, when people readily believe that animal bones show evidence that the animals were eaten, those same people, when shown human bones bearing identical evidence, reject the obvious conclusion.

It is true that in spite of the care Turner has taken over the presentation of his conclusions, a number of scientists are still not convinced. In fact, some believe that Turner is not merely wrong but that he is inflicting a new and terrible violence on Native Americans.

Kurt Dongoske, a white man who is a Hopi tribe archaeologist, believes Turner's findings diminish the human character of the Anasazi and, by association, the Hopi themselves:

Just to call somebody a cannibal is dehumanizing; it makes them less human than you are. There is a long tradition in the United States of science trying to dehumanize Native Americans. I'm not saying that Christy Turner is consciously doing that, but I think when the idea of cannibalism is picked up by the media it takes on a life of its own. It becomes fact, and it has that consequence of dehumanizing Native American populations, particularly Hopi.

Bruce Bradley shares some of Kurt Dongoske's misgivings. The Pueblo people and other Native Americans find it very difficult to deal with the findings of Turner's research, he says, because to talk in generalities is dehumanizing. As he sees it, the jury is still out on whether violence really played a major role in the Chacoan system:

Certainly there are some aberrations. They can happen in any society, any family – how do you determine if something is domestic violence or institutional? As for south-western archaeology, I'd estimate less than a tenth of a per cent of what happened in the past is known. The truth is, when you come right down to it, we make a lot of noise about how much evidence we have, but we have diddly-squat.

If many scientists and Native Americans are offended by Turner's theories, it is because of the enormity of the implications. The Anasazi have been the most historically revered of all the inhabitants of the American South-West; Turner claims his evidence shows that they practised cannibalism at a time and place that marked the very peak of their civilization.

The Anasazi prospered from roughly AD 900 to 1150. Their sphere of influence spread outwards from Chaco Canyon and spanned an area bigger than Ireland. A network of 9-metre-wide roads stretched across the canyon lands, linking the Anasazi's great houses – more than 150 of them. Around their altars and hearths hundreds of people would have gathered for sacred rituals. And it's there and at that time, in the time of the flowering of Anasazi culture, that Turner believes cannibalism took place.

'It's really a very sensitive subject,' said Kurt Dongoske. 'He is so removed from it. It's so abstract for him. How can he possibly understand the sensitivity of it?' Turner's rebuttal is measured and calm:

> I think the people who would say I'm insensitive know nothing about me. We're not insensitive to this. What we are insensitive to is that we're not being politically correct. Being politically correct is *not* doing science. Science finds the truth, and it takes the community to deal with that truth. I think we've found the truth.

Across the Chaco region Turner examined remains from almost eighty sites, and he is satisfied that he found clear evidence of cannibalism in roughly half of them. That means, in all, nearly three hundred human beings killed and eaten. If Turner's findings were to be widely accepted, it would mean a grim reversal of the Anasazi's benign image: he is asking society to accept a history of massacres and cannibalism all the way from Wupatki, on the western edge of Chaco, to Salmon Ruin on the north. And even in Chaco Canyon itself, at Pueblo Bonito – which was perhaps the ceremonial centre of the Chaco world – time and again Turner found the signature of cannibalism. 'We didn't want to destroy the myth of Chaco Canyon,' he said. 'But we had to find an objective explanation for this damage to human remains. Everything that we have done meets any scientific requirement. There is no other explanation.'

By most scientific standards Turner had his proof, hundreds of sets of human remains that were carved in exactly the same way as game. But some doubters still argued that the proof was not complete: a critical link was missing, for while Turner's studies presented clear and multiple evidence of human butchering, his detractors demanded hard evidence that the human meat had actually been eaten.

A few archaeologists and anthropologists suggested that the game-like processing of the bodies might be attributable to other cultural practices, such as burial ceremonies or the ritual mutilation of enemies or witches. As Kurt Dongoske said:

> People kill each other all the time. They don't always eat each other. If you kill somebody, you're either doing it out of self-defence or aggression, or protecting something. When you go to the extent of eating somebody, you are pushed to a more extreme point. It's one thing to say that the bones were disarticulated and butchered; it's another thing to say that the flesh was consumed. That's a big leap.

But in 1997 a critical piece of evidence turned up in a remote south-west corner of Colorado. At an Anasazi site known as Cowboy Wash, excavators led by Professor Brian Billman of the University of North Carolina found the skeletons of twenty-four people, nearly a third of the estimated population. There was persuasive evidence that the bodies had been chopped and cooked. And they found something else. In the hearth of a kiva, at the centre of the community, an insult had been left: it was a coprolite, a mound of fossilized human faeces.

Professor Billman found the implications of the discovery exciting. If the coprolite could be shown to have come from a cannibal, then he and his team might well have uncovered the final proof of Turner's theory.

Evaluating the evidence was a matter for molecular biochemistry. Richard Marlar, a biochemist and an associate professor of pathology at the University of Colorado Health Sciences Center in Denver, is an expert on blood as well as being an amateur archaeologist. He was fascinated by the challenge presented by the coprolite. He knew that up to the time when he was prepared to test for a proof of cannibalism, the scientific argument for cannibalism was in a position agonizingly short of closure:

> We were able to say, OK, the individuals were probably violently killed. Their bones and bodies had been processed. That all suggests cannibalism, but it doesn't prove it. The point is, then, we can follow the concept of cannibalism all the way up to the mouth of the suspects, but you can't prove that they truly ate human flesh.

Marlar set out to find the proof, to identify the residue of one human in the excrement of another. But what kind of test would prove that? It was a scientific challenge that had never been confronted before. 'We had to find a protein that was only found in human skeletal muscle,' said Marlar. 'Muscles of the legs or the arms, not any kind found in the gut.'

That protein was myoglobin. It functions as a unit of oxygen storage and provides oxygen on demand to the working muscles. 'Human myoglobin could only show up in someone's faeces one way,' explained Marlar: 'if he had consumed a person.'

He prepared his test with the utmost care. There could be no risking the production of false positives for animal myoglobin, or for other human proteins that might have entered the intestinal tract. First he tested the stools of many of his patients from the hospital where he works, verifying that none contained traces of myoglobin.

After months of preparation, months of blocking off avenues of possible error and of refining the test procedure, all was ready. Marlar set up an immunological trial, the kind usually employed to determine whether a person has a disease. He carried out seven tests, each in triplicate, using twenty-one fragments of the coprolite. He also ran six tests on the ceramic pottery to determine if it contained traces of human protein from cooking.

The results, in liquid form, were to be colour-coded: blue meant no human remains in the coprolite or the pottery, but if any of the specimens from the coprolite turned yellow, it would be irrefutable evidence of the consumption of human muscle tissue.

Marlar ran the tests over a period of several weeks. Time after time the results came back the same: yellow, positive for human myoglobin. 'We did find human myoglobin in the coprolite,' Marlar said, adding that it had been present in the interior walls of the cooking pot, too.

He was now satisfied that human tissue had been eaten and passed through another human system at Cowboy Wash. Consumption had at last been confirmed. Cannibalism among the Anasazi had been demonstrated beyond doubt.

All over the world, growing numbers of scientists are now using Turner's methods to re-evaluate data from earlier discoveries. Researchers recently found signs of cannibalism in Spain from 800,000 years ago. At Gough's cave in Somerset, an excavation begun in the late 1980s, led by anthropologist Chris Stringer, uncovered a discarded pile of bones roughly 12,000 years old. Many were animal bones, but among them were human bones, too. They were taken to the Natural History Museum in London, where Peter Andrews, an evolutionary anthropologist, and biopalaeontologist Yolanda Fernandez-

Jalvo began a year-long analysis. Selected fragments of bone were subjected to minute examination using one of the most sophisticated pieces of modern technology available for the purpose: the scanning electron microscope.

In the basic electron microscope, instead of light being used, a stream of electrons is aimed at the object under examination; electrons have a much shorter wavelength than light, so much more detailed images and higher magnifications are possible than with conventional microscopes. In electron microscopes the 'lenses' are in fact magnets that focus the electron beam so that it does not deviate. In a scanning electron microscope, which is designed for the detailed examination of solid objects, a beam of electrons is swept across the target object. The microscope produces a finely detailed image at a predetermined magnification by converting the feedback data from the electrons – known as backscatter – into a picture on a computer screen.

In the laboratory at the Natural History Museum, specimen after specimen was scanned at a magnification of 1,000 times. The bone surfaces showed unmistakable markings from stone tools – in fact, the marks left by those nomadic Stone Age hunter-gatherers were almost identical to those left by the Anasazi in Chaco Canyon. This was a discovery that suggests that prehistoric cannibalism was more common than had been previously suspected.

'Probably all populations, all races, all people, at one stage or another, have practised cannibalism,' said Peter Andrews. 'It's a very characteristic thing about being human. Are we prepared to accept that our ancestors were cannibals?'

If scientists were now beginning to see cannibalism as a characteristic running through long tracts of humanity's early history, the next question was: why? In Africa, Spain and Great Britain, the answer appeared to be that people ate other people because they were short of alternative sources of food. The mix of human and animal bones in the same rubbish heaps pointed to hunger as the driving force.

Speculation over what brought cannibalism to Chaco Canyon, however, did not provide investigators with ready answers, even though the basic facts were clear enough: 15,000 skeletons, 500 with signs of violent death, another 300 butchered and consumed – statistically one in fifty were victims of cannibalism. The cases included men, women, children and even the unborn. What was the cause? Not hunger. It is the oldest reason for humans to eat their own kind, but dendrochronology showed that, during the period in question, the Anasazi were unlikely to have experienced famine, or even any milder forms of dietary hardship.

Dendrochronology, is a method of dating and interpreting past events, particularly climatic trends, based on the analysis of tree rings. Samples are obtained with an increment borer, a small-bore metal tube that can be driven into a tree to get a core sample that extends from the bark to the centre. In the laboratory the sample is split and the rings are counted and measured. The sequence of the rings is compared with sequences from other core samples. The technique relies on the fact that many tree species produce growth rings during their annual growing seasons. The amount of annual growth is determined by various factors, but it tends to fluctuate in proportion to either the amount of available rain or the prevailing temperatures. Ring measurements made from trees with overlapping ages can provide climate information going back thousands of years.

Tree-ring dating showed that in the American South-West the years 900 to 1150 were marked by a warming trend. Food was easier to cultivate, game was easier to catch. It was a time of plenty, so in Chaco Canyon starvation as a cause of cannibalism was unlikely. Even so, Harvard archaeologist Steven LeBlanc made some grisly calculations.

The average event seems to represent maybe five or seven people, but some of them seem to represent perhaps thirty people. And those are the hardest to explain. The number of people it would have taken to consume thirty individuals is really staggering: maybe two to four hundred people. You try to compute just how much would have been consumed in one of these events. It turns out to be hundreds of pounds of meat.

That's too many people and too much food at any one time for the starvation theory to make sense. Warfare was at the core of another theory. According to LeBlanc there is evidence of warfare throughout the ancient South-West.

People were really being killed. There really were massacres. But during the two and a half centuries of the Chaco phenomenon, things were different. You have this fairly long period of 800, 1,000 years up to about AD 900, with this chronic, intermittent warfare. And then, almost suddenly, it stops, and you see this period of about 200, 250 years with virtually no warfare. So it's this 200-year interval that really is so enigmatic. Although it was a time of peace, that's precisely the time when cannibalism did occur.

So war was not a factor, either. What was left? The enigma persisted until Turner and his colleagues, pondering connections and influences, began to discern a pattern.

Dr David Wilcox, of the Museum of Northern Arizona, commented: 'It was very interesting to see that, indeed, almost all of Turner's cases of what he thinks are cannibalistic events fall within the distribution zone of the Chacoan great houses, and they fall in time from about 900 to 1150 – that is, the time of the Chacoan phenomenon.'

Nearly all of the excavated great houses show signs of violent disorder, and two-thirds bear evidence of cannibalism. Close to ninety per cent of the instances of cannibalism were committed either in or near the Chacoan great houses. This realization was a breakthrough, indicating that Chaco's great houses and the practice of cannibalism were inextricably linked.

Turner and others suspected the involvement of outside influences. The architecture of the great houses bears traces of cultures far to the south, from Meso-America – a region from northern Mexico to Nicaragua, which had been civilized in pre-Spanish times. The influences were reminiscent of the cultures of the Toltecs and other ancient peoples from the area known today as the Valley of Mexico. Below the Chaco great house of Wupatki in north-central Arizona there is a ball-game court, which was an integral part of Meso-American culture. Throughout Chaco Canyon itself, the ruins suggested to Turner a Meso-American influence, especially at Chetro Kettl, the largest of the great houses:

> It has a wall that runs a city block at least, with columns in it that are exactly like the columns you see in many Meso-American sites. Some time after they built those columns, somebody filled those things in to make a façade. But initially, in the early part of that construction, it was like nothing that had occurred in the South-West previously.

Although Turner had long been aware of the Meso-American features in and around the Chacoan great houses, it was only now, with the established connection between the great houses and cannibalism, that he suspected a powerful significance in the influences from the south. 'This was so big,' he said. 'When I looked at this stuff, I saw something that was so much bigger than local evolution could have possibly produced. This is something that *came in*.'

Turner was searching for a clue more significant than Meso-American influences in the architecture. He needed evidence that people themselves had come up from the south. Perhaps, he thought, there were clues in the skeletal remains:

> We looked all over the potential kinds of evidence we could find and then – eureka! We could identify Mexicans by their modified teeth. In the Valley of Mexico and throughout Meso-America, people modify their teeth by chipping, filing, inlaying, drilling them and doing all kinds of things to them. So if we have got some individuals here in the South-West with dental modifications, the odds are very good that they are from Mexico, because there is no tradition of tooth modification in California, the Great Basin, the Rocky Mountains, the South-West, the great plains, you name it.

Re-examining the bones from Pueblo Bonito in Chaco Canyon for the fifth time, Turner found what he was looking for. It was a skull originally discovered by Neil M. Judd in 1954 in Room 330 of Pueblo Bonito; it was a man's skull, and the upper front teeth had been deliberately chipped and notched to create a decorative effect.

'I think we've got the direct link between Meso-America and the South-West. So what do I see? I've got a Mexican over here with chipped teeth, I've got victims of cannibalism in three or four rooms over in the same place. I see Mexico.'

The connection that Turner perceived is to be found in today's Mexico City, once the capital of a vast Meso-American empire, where echoes of a vanished society provide a persuasive solution to the arrival and practice of cannibalism in Chaco Canyon. Templo Mayor, an immense ceremonial complex of stepped temples and huge altars, is a ruin now, but once it was the religious centre of a culture with a spiritual commitment to ceremonial sacrifice and the ritual eating of human beings.

The island where the Aztecs built their capital – which they called Tenochtitlán – quickly grew into the largest and most influential empire in Meso-America. The island is now Mexico City's central area, and the Plaza Mayor, now called Zócala (its official name is the Plaza de la Constitución), lies at the very centre of the city, surrounded by bustling streets.

Although the Aztec culture flourished in the fifteenth and sixteenth centuries, they claimed descendancy from the Toltecs, reputed to be the original civilizing influence of Meso-America. The Aztecs perpetuated a great deal of the religious philosophy of the Toltecs and other early cultures of Meso-America; historically, they have stood as the archetype of a culture that extended the boundaries of torture, human sacrifice and cannibalism in the service of their many gods. It is correct to say that the Aztecs owed the worst aspects of their history to the religious brutalities inherited through their descendancy from the Toltecs.

A brief look at Toltec culture shows us the kind of influence that Professor Turner believes brought cannibalism to the Anasazi. Traditional texts call the Toltecs the prime civilizers, ruling a vast empire from their capital city, Tula (sometimes given as Tollan). Legend has it that the Toltecs were the first builders of cities, the original astrologers and the developers of myriad advanced crafts. Three big questions hang over the Toltecs' history. Did they really exist? Where was Tula? Did the Toltecs really achieve the remarkable political and civilizing feats that the annals describe? The annals themselves are contradictory about dates and the successions of kings. Three notable chronologies of the Toltec empire have survived. The dates given by Ixtlilxóchitl, a scholarly mestizo (a person of mixed Spanish and Native American blood), put the Toltecs well within the Classic period of Meso-American development – AD 100 to 600 – but the others position them in the earlier part of the Post-Classic period, from AD 900 to 1519. The majority of informed historians and other commentators are inclined to accept the later dates, but that would disqualify the Toltecs as being the first civilized peoples in central Mexico, which is what their histories claim.

As for the majestic city of Tula, most historians who actually believe in it favour an archaeological site near the present-day town of Tula, situated in Hidalgo state in east-central Mexico. However, a number of investigators have rejected that site in favour of Teotihuacán, near Mexico City. As with the Toltecs themselves, vagueness surrounds the historical records of their capital city, and there are plentiful contradictions about people and events. But in spite of conflicts and doubts, persistent historical references to the Toltecs, their empire and the great city of Tula indicate that substantial historical truth is buried beneath the confusion. Archaeologists in general accept that the Toltecs did occupy a significant place in the history of Meso-America.

No one doubts that the Aztecs existed; no one doubts, either, that they believed the Toltecs were their forebears and that the terrifying rituals they indulged in had been handed down intact from the prime movers at Tula.

The stones of Templo Mayor are decorated with sculptures depicting angry, vindictive gods, some with human faces, others with the heads of serpents and demons from darkest fantasy; they depict natural forces, violent and randomly destructive deities, demanding to be appeased. The images are persistently grotesque – the God and Goddess of Death are stark-eyed figures with exposed ribcages. Aztec religion placed extreme emphasis on sacrifice through blood-letting and the ceremonial killing of people. The surviving images in Templo Mayor make one realize the sheer intensity of their belief. In the preserved histories of the Aztecs, known as the codices, there are repeated tales of dismemberment, decapitation and the boiling of bodies. Spanish records describe horrendous ceremonies at which thousands of sacrificial captives would be bent backwards over a stone slab and have knives plunged into their chests. Their hearts, still beating, were torn from the cavity of the chest, held aloft in tribute to whatever god was being appeased, then dropped into a vast ceremonial vessel. The records state that portions of the dead bodies were eaten by priests and votaries. Evidence also suggests that the remainder of the sacrificial victims' bodies were sold at special markets, where they were bought to be eaten in the belief that the act of cannibalism would impart health and vigour not otherwise attainable.

Hundreds of years later the bones of many of the victims ended up in the National Museum of Anthropology and History in Mexico City. The collection houses 20,000 skeletal remains excavated from 600 archaeological sites in Mexico.

Physical anthropologist Carmen Pijoan has carried out extensive taphonomic studies on Meso-American bones dating from at least 500 BC. Her examination of the bones has revealed evidence of extremely savage treatment. She has found signs of ritual cannibalism and other equally grotesque practices. 'They thought about using the body of the sacrifice victims in any way they could,' she said. 'Bones were crafted into tools and ornaments. Longer bones from arms and legs were made into ritual musical instruments.'

Deep parallel cuts were made along the shafts of long bones, creating a row of notches. A stick or another bone could be drawn across the top of the notches to create a rhythmic rasping sound. Skulls were put to extraordinary uses, too. 'A hole was punched very carefully on the bottom of the skull,' Pijoan said, 'and the skull was afterwards put on a pole as a trophy.'

Multiple skulls made fairly typical Meso-American trophies. Holes were punched on either side of each skull, then the skulls were lined up side by side, sometimes dozens of them. Next, a long pole was passed through the line of skulls from one end to the other and fixed in place; the skulls could then be displayed in a grimacing row, without any danger that one or more would come loose and spoil the display. In one find, a skull-rack of this kind consisted of 170 skulls. The purpose of such displays was probably to frighten people and forestall any chance of resistance to the all-powerful priesthood.

Human sacrifice itself was a cohesive factor in the society of the Meso-Americans. It preserved the theocracy – the rule by priests on behalf of the savage gods – and it thereby secured the position of those in power, the very ones who claimed only to pass on the punitive, repressive doctrines of higher beings.

But just before the start of the Chaco era, civil unrest shook this world. The codices say that many people fled north, away from Mexico. Professor Turner's theory is that a small cult travelled north to Chaco Canyon, bringing their cult of blood with them. He believes that when this tough, manipulative group came across the Anasazi, they found themselves in the presence of peaceful and therefore pliant people. In Turner's view, it was cultists from Mexico, keen to re-establish themselves in a position of power, who set out to duplicate the system of dominance by terror they had left behind:

> They needed some kind of weapon, and certainly cannibalism would serve as a weapon. You don't have to kill a lot of people to make your point. And they used cannibalism as a threat. It's a terrifying thing; we're afraid of it ourselves. The revulsion is because we can imagine it. I can imagine word getting out that we've got cannibals in our midst. It would bring about a lot of social control with very, very little effort.

Turner now suggests that the Anasazi, far from being the perpetrators of cannibalism, were in fact its victims, a view endorsed by David Wilcox of the Museum of Northern Arizona:

> I think the terrorism idea, in one form or another, in my mind, is the strongest hypothesis we have. If it's people treating other people as though they're animals, and butchering them in the same way that you would an animal, and even consuming the result, that probably is intended to send a political message.

This oppressive regime held sway for at least two and a half centuries. Then some time close to the year 1150, changes began to occur. The dendrochronological record shows that the climate became considerably colder and drier. Crops would have begun to fail, and game animals would have become scarce. Drought came, and with it starvation, disease and an inevitable reduction in numbers of the living. The Chaco system collapsed. The evidence of the bones is that just at this time, cannibalism in the lands of the Anasazi began to disappear, too.

It is comforting to assume that not just the climatic changes but a spiritual revival among the ancient people caused them to turn away from the barbarism of their oppressors. The fact is that we do not know what happened. We cannot know for sure.

An ancient Native American story says that Chaco once became a place of evil and that something terrible happened at that place. This evil, the story ran, threw the world out of balance. For centuries the story was no more than folklore without substantial backing from the history of the region. Now, the clear evidence uncovered by Professor Christy Turner and others lends compelling support to the legend.

3

THE LOST
VIKINGS

GREENLAND IS A VAST, forbidding region of ice and darkness, described in the Oxford English Dictionary as 'a large island or small continent to the north-east of North America'. Nowadays it is generally accepted that Greenland is the world's largest island, extending 2,670 kilometres north to south, and rather more than 1,050 kilometres east to west at its widest point. The coastline is deeply indented and is nearly 40,000 kilometres long, which roughly equals the circumference of the earth at the equator. A 180-metre-deep submarine shelf connects Greenland to North America, which makes it effectively an extension of the rock mass that supports Canada, known as the Canadian Shield.

The island's ice sheet is its most striking physical feature, second only in size to the one that covers Antarctica. The average thickness of the sheet is 1,500 metres, reaching over 3,000 metres in places. The only parts on the island free of ice are coastal areas, most of them highlands. Nowadays an estimated 55,000 people, in many small coastal communities, make an arduous living from fishing and mining.

Pointers to a mystery from Greenland's medieval past lie at the heart of the present-day settlements and on Greenland's eastern coastline. Although no more than a few stones remain as signs of a vanished culture, over 1,000 years ago Vikings went there, established their own settlement and stayed for more than 500 years. During that time they prospered, establishing a way of life that incorporated some of the signal features of medieval Europe. And then, quite suddenly it seemed, their settlements disappeared one by one. The question of what happened to the Vikings has perplexed and fascinated generations of scientists and historians.

'The colony in Greenland finally disappears from history in about the year 1500,' said historian Dr Judith Jesch of the University of Nottingham. 'Nobody knows exactly why or exactly when this happened. It's one of the great unsolved mysteries of the Middle Ages.'

The first Vikings to disappear had settled close to a fjord on Greenland's west coast. In approximately the year 1340, an emissary from Norway, Ivar Bardarson, sailed into the fjord and went ashore to visit the Western Settlement. What he found troubled him. The place was deserted. He was the only human there. In his report he noted, 'I saw nobody, neither Christians nor heathens, only some wild cattle and sheep, all running wild.' The Vikings of the Western Settlement seemed to have disappeared overnight. One hundred and sixty years later similar sudden disappearences happened to the other two settlements, and by 1500 there were no Vikings left. 'The Norse Greenlanders had left or died out,' noted Dr Jesch, 'probably fairly recently, since the domestic animals were still there.'

The story of Bardarson's discovery of the deserted settlement has since sent ripples of speculation through academic and scientific communities. Down the centuries successive generations have pondered the enigma: what could have happened to cause a once prosperous culture to vanish, and so suddenly?

Fully 650 years after the event, scientists from Scandinavia, Britain and the United States are working in Greenland with a view to finding the answer. They are chemists, physicists, botanists and archaeologists, who are pooling their resources and bringing their individual strains of expertise to the job of cracking the mystery. One of them is Dr Bent Fredskild, a botanist who has been intrigued with the case of the lost Vikings for over forty years. As he explained:

> It's a long story. It started in 1955, on my first visit, and since then I've spent twenty-nine whole summers in different places in Greenland. The main topics of my work have been to study the present flora – flowering plants and grasses, etc. – to study their distribution all over Greenland and their relation to the climate. The other topic I've worked with is the history of vegetation and thereby the history of the climate, since the last glaciation 10,000 to 12,000 years ago.

Away from its little towns, Greenland has no roads, so the scientists had to make their various journeys as the Vikings did, by boat. A Viking farmstead in a remote coastal valley was a key archaeological site. One team was led by Dr Jette Arneborg of the National Museum of Denmark, who remarked that every new generation has new answers to the question of what happened to the Norse Greenlanders. 'I think that's very exciting,' she said, 'and in a way it reflects that history is very much alive in our society today.'

Arneborg's team planned to camp at the farmstead site for a month and take advantage of the Arctic summer, which lasts only a few weeks. They set to work as soon as they arrived, knowing from experience just where to start searching for clues – a medieval midden, or rubbish dump. They dug their way down through the hardened peat and soil, cutting a trench in which they could move freely and examine the strata revealed on the sides. Every farmstead had a midden, and generations of farmers and their families made it the repository for everything they discarded, such things as leftover bones from meals, old toys, broken furniture and general farmhouse refuse. Every object the investigators found could be dated, because they were able to work out when individual layers of the midden had been established. Jens Fog Jensen of the Danish Polar Centre explained:

> The very top of the trench side is a layer that just came on a few years ago, and then beneath this we have a recent peat layer. And then there is the first Norse layer, which has a lot of charcoal and bone remains in it. The Viking period is actually documented all the way from the bottom until fifteen centimetres below the recent surface.

As the days passed, the findings from the excavation helped the team assemble an increasingly clearer picture of life in that place at the peak of the farmstead's prosperity. Judith Jesch has contributed further information from the surviving documents and sagas of the period. A saga, in the context of medieval Nordic literature, means broadly any kind of story or historical record presented in prose. 'The earliest and most reliable source tells us of a man called Erik the Red from Norway who heard of a country to the west and sailed to find it,' she said. 'He discovered it and called it Greenland, then later went back with twenty-five ships of settlers.'

Erik the Red was the byname of Erik Thorvaldson, the father of Leif Eriksson, who was one of the first Europeans to arrive in North America. Erik left his native Norway when he was a child of eight, accompanied by his father, Thorvald, who had been exiled temporarily by the Norwegian authorities for manslaughter. The pair went to live in Iceland, and it was there, in his youth, that Erik was given the nickname of Erik the Red – the reason is not known. In early manhood (accounts vary, but most say he was twenty-two) Erik was sentenced to three years' exile from Iceland for manslaughter, a stroke of coincidence more remarkable than most.

He decided to spend his time of banishment exploring the land to the west. The vast ice-coated island, as yet without a name, lay across 280 kilometres of ocean and was just visible from the tops of mountains in western Iceland. Erik sailed in 982 with his household and livestock, but because of gigantic ice drifts he could not get near the eastern coast of the forbidding landmass. He and several adventurous companions sailed round the southern tip of the island and finally settled in an area near the present-day township of Julianehåb. In the three years of Erik's exile, neither he nor any of his comrades saw or heard any other people.

Erik returned to Iceland in 986, where his enthusiastic descriptions of the new territory convinced a considerable number of people that a better life waited for them elsewhere. According to an ancient Nordic record called *Islendingabók*, Erik gave the island the name of Greenland, 'because it would induce settlers to go there, if the land had a good name'.

Twenty-five ships of would-be settlers sailed from Iceland, but only fourteen ships and 350 colonists are recorded landing at a place later named Eystribygdh, 'the Eastern Colony'. By the year 1000 there were estimated to be 1,000 Scandinavian settlers in the colony, but an epidemic in 1002 cut down the population considerably. Erik's colony, which is celebrated in the Icelandic *Erik the Red's Saga*, gradually faded away.

Other settlements thrived. These Greenland Vikings were farmers who lived in buildings made from turf, stone and timber in the style of their Scandinavian ancestors. 'They lived in small, isolated farmhouses,' languages (etymologists now believe the word is Old English in origin and was only later adopted by the Scandinavians).

Although the ethnic make-up of many individual Viking armies is not recorded, their numbers in the Viking expansion in Russia and in the Baltic are known to have been mainly Swedish. On the other hand, the relatively peaceful takeover of the Faeroes, the Orkneys and Iceland was certainly the work of Norwegians.

In the late eighth century there were a number of sporadic, capricious Viking raids on English seaboard towns. Then in 865 the raids suddenly turned more frequent and a good deal harsher. A marauding band led by the sons of Ragnar Lodbrok – Healfdene, Inwaer and Hubba – conquered the old kingdoms of East Anglia and Northumbria. They also burned Mercia to a quarter of its previous size.

Generally the Vikings swept all before them, but for some reason they couldn't overthrow the Wessex of Alfred the Great, and although he was put under tremendous pressure by constantly replenished Viking armies, Alfred finally beat them. The morale of the old Anglo-Saxon kingdom was restored and possibly surpassed. Alfred's son, Edward the Elder, and his army promptly took on the task of liberating England from the grip of the Danes.

It was a long, drawn-out campaign, but before Edward's death in 924 he had defeated the Danish states on Mercian and East Anglian territory. The remote Northumbria held out longer, but Scandinavian control there was finally smashed by Edred in 954. In 980 Viking attacks on England flared up again, and the country became part of the empire of Canute, a Dane, in 1016. English control, nevertheless, was restored peacefully in 1042, and the Viking threat ended with Canute II's feeble attempts at invasion in the reign of William I. The Scandinavian conquests in England were over, but they left permanent marks in the social fabric, in the language, in place names and in personal names.

said Judith Jesch, 'and you have to remember that it was dark for most of the year that far north, so they would sit indoors and amuse themselves by composing poetry, telling stories, carving toys out of wood and ivory, and playing chess, perhaps.'

The Vikings, by that time, were a civilized people, vastly different from the horde of marauders who had first taken the name.

The Vikings, also called Norsemen and Northmen, were seafaring Scandinavian warriors who invaded, ransacked and colonized large areas of Europe for more than two hundred years. They were active from the late eighth to the mid-eleventh centuries, and their turbulent, murderous ambitions had a profound effect on the history of Europe. In the view of many historians these pagan Danes, Norwegians and Swedes were motivated by factors that ranged from overpopulation in their countries of origin to the comparative weakness of the people they chose to victimize.

In cross-section the Vikings were landowning chieftains, heads of clans, retainers, freemen, plus any clan members who wanted a life of adventure and were fit enough for the challenge it offered. At home these men were mostly self-reliant farmers; once they took to the high seas they became a collective of warriors, a bloody-handed menace to any civilized community worth raiding. The record shows that in the Viking era Scandinavia appears to have had a nearly endless supply of fighting men. There was no shortage, either, of natural leaders who could muster and train bands of warriors, and even armies, with a degree of speed and thoroughness that has probably never been surpassed. These uncommonly hostile invaders, described by the nineteenth-century historian George Stephens as 'an unbearable curse', would cross the seas in their longships and make hit-and-run attacks on European coastal communities. Their plundering and killing earned them the name 'vikingr', a word that means 'pirate' in the early Scandinavian

Scandinavian expansionism touched countless places on its move westwards. Settlers poured into Iceland from at least the year 900, and during the same century the first colonies from Iceland were established in Greenland; colonization into North America was also attempted. Over the same period, settlements appeared in the Orkneys, the Faeroes, the Shetland Isles, the Hebrides and the Isle of Man.

Scandinavian invasions of Ireland have been recorded from 795, when Rechru (an island that historians have not been able to identify) was pillaged, ransacked and its three communities burned. From that point onwards, fighting was non-stop, and although from time to time the natives held their own, Scandinavian kingdoms were established in Dublin, Limerick and Waterford. A curiosity not adequately explained in the history books is that for a time in the early tenth century the kings of Dublin ruled in both Dublin and Northumberland. In 1014 the chance of Ireland being unified under the Scandinavians vanished on the battlefield of Clontarf, where the Irish Scandinavians, backed by the forces of the Earl of Orkney and a few native Irish, were heavily defeated. Nevertheless, the twelfth-century English invaders of Ireland found the Scandinavians still in a commanding position (though now they were Christians) at Dublin, Waterford, Limerick, Wexford and Cork.

The Viking imprint was never to be as pronounced elsewhere as it was in the British Isles. Apart from in Normandy, the Scandinavian influence on languages and customs in mainland Europe is very slight. Until the end of the Viking period, some raiding *did* take place, and tenth-century Viking settlements along the River Seine were the nucleus of the duchy of Normandy. The Vikings also carried out occasional raids in Spain and the Mediterranean coasts, but practically nothing permanent was established.

History shows us that the Viking expansion to the east was probably less of a bludgeoning process than it had been on the Atlantic coasts. In the Baltic there was considerable spasmodic raiding, but no Viking strongholds were ever established in that region. The most impressive expansion took the Scandinavians into the heart of Russia, where at one time they dominated, among other places, Novgorod and Kiev. They were, however, quickly assimilated into the native population, to whom they gave their name of 'Rus' – Russians.

The Rus were mainly traders, and a couple of their trading agreements with the Greeks have survived in the Russian *Primary Chronicle* for the years 912 and 945; the Rus traders who signed the agreements have decidedly Scandinavian names. Occasionally, the Rus attempted voyages of plunder like their kinsmen in the west, but their existence as a separate people did not continue past 1050 at the latest.

There was apparently a new Viking movement eastwards during the early years of the eleventh century: runic stones from Sweden list the names of men who went with Yngvarr on his journeys to the East, but there is no historical record of why they went. Hundreds of Scandinavians travelled eastwards at that time to serve as mercenaries; many of them went to Constantinople, now Istanbul, where they became the Varangian Guard of the Byzantine Empire.

After the eleventh century, Norway and Sweden had lost the strength and the numbers to make further conquering forays abroad. Denmark, on the other hand, continued to dragoon the excess of young and energetic Danish men into powerful royal armies, which sailed the seas in search of further conquest. But the years of arrogant dominance by the Viking chiefs were over.

The Greenland Vikings usually built their homes and farm buildings in sheltered valleys tucked among the hills; sheep, cattle and goats imported from Scandinavia were kept in specially erected compounds.

Signs of age and expansion in the ruins demonstrate that over the years the population grew steadily. Before they vanished, there were probably 6,000 Vikings living in Greenland.

In winter, because of the incredibly low temperatures, the Vikings kept their animals indoors with them and shared their heat. Because the animals could not exercise in the cramped confines of the family dwellings, they would soon have lost the power of their legs. Records of the same thing happening – often over much shorter winters – survive from civilizations around the world, and they are remarkably consistent in their details. When spring came, the animals would have to be carried out to the fields to graze and gradually regain the strength in their limbs. Judith Jesch described the Vikings' lifestyle:

> The Vikings lived by subsistence agriculture in Greenland, and they had to import a lot of the things that were necessary to their lifestyle. They had to bring in timber for the housing, they had to import iron for the nails to build the houses. In order to get these from abroad, for instance from Norway, they exported Greenland falcons, which were known as far away as Sicily. They exported walrus ivory, which in the early Middle Ages was the only source of the commodity. It was exported throughout Europe and carved into beautiful objects found in churches ... crucifixes, caskets and the like.

The settlers thrived for 500 years. The income from trading paid for sturdy, comfortable dwellings and magnificent churches; the Vikings even sent a message to the Pope asking him to appoint their own bishop, and in exchange they offered the gift of a polar bear.

But this flowering of their culture failed. We know that in the fourteenth and fifteenth centuries something probably unforeseen hit the fabric of Greenland Viking society. As Judith Jesch put it:

> The last known communication from Norse Greenland was in the year 1408. A party of Icelanders arrived in Norway, having come from Greenland. While they were there, two of them decided to get married, and we have very detailed records of the wedding that took place in the church at Hvalsey on 16 September 1408. The record says that there were many people there, both Greenlanders of Viking descent, and foreigners.

It was all done with Christian propriety, Judith Jesch added. The banns, for instance, were read out in church for three consecutive weeks before the wedding. But the wedding wasn't the only distraction for the visiting Icelanders while they were in Greenland. 'A man called Kollgrim apparently seduced a married woman using witchcraft and black arts and was sentenced to death by burning at the stake. The woman he seduced never really recovered from this experience, and she died shortly afterwards.'

Following that report from the Icelanders, nothing further was heard about the Greenland Vikings.

Artefacts from the excavations were the only guides available to the archaeologists. Deduction from the accumulated evidence, with every scientist contributing his and her interpretations, was the only procedure likely to yield worthwhile answers. That would take time, but for the moment there was no harm in theorizing.

'One possibility is the plague, that they died of illness and the colony was just wiped out,' Judith Jesch postulated. 'Another possibility is that they were kidnapped by pirates. It's also been suggested that they intermarried with the Inuit, the native Greenlanders.'

Other investigators have suggested that the Vikings perished in a war with the Inuit. The ancient records of Arctic history tell of battles lost, in one of them the chronicler claiming that eighteen Vikings were killed.

Pioneering excavations in the early 1900s provided other valuable leads. Graves in Greenland's Viking churchyards were excavated and the bones removed; farmhouse middens, too, surrendered a wealth of artefacts. The early digs even uncovered medieval clothes, preserved in the permafrost, their shape and colours intact. Eighty years on, new clues to the disappearance of the settlers were uncovered by a renewed and better-informed inspection of the graveyard bones.

In the Laboratory of Biological Anthropology at the University of Copenhagen, where the early finds are now archived, pathologist Dr Niels Lynnerup studied the skeletons using forensic techniques. He made an outstanding discovery: during the final years of the settlements, the Vikings' life expectancy shrank significantly. In Dr Lynnerup's view, this was the result of a dramatic decline in people's health and living conditions:

> We have the remains of three hundred and fifty Norse. The average life span was about thirty to thirty-five years. I would think maybe there was a decline throughout the settlement period. People would be living maybe to thirty-five years old and then gradually the life span fell by a couple of years throughout the five hundred years of settlement.

While searching for signs of an illness that might have shortened the Vikings' lives, Dr Lynnerup examined a series of X-rays of the skulls and made another crucial discovery. 'We found that there was a higher frequency of middle-ear disease in the later settlement period compared with the early settlement period.'

This was a clear sign that the Vikings' health had deteriorated. To understand why Dr Lynnerup attached this significance to the discovery, it is useful to know a little about the ear and its special proneness to disease in undernourished people.

The outer ear is an efficient funnel-like structure that carries sound directly to the eardrum, which vibrates and transmits the waves to the middle ear. The middle ear is air-filled and has three tiny bones, called ossicles, which interact and not only pass on sound from the eardrum to the fluid-filled inner ear but actually amplify the vibrations. The inner ear contains the cochlea, a winding cone-shaped tube that resembles a snail's shell: this is the organ of hearing. The amplified vibrations from the middle ear stimulate small hairs inside the cochlea, which causes impulses to be sent along the auditory nerve to the brain. The semicircular canals, the organs that give us our sense of orientation and balance, are also housed in the inner ear.

The ear, then, is an efficient, sophisticated organ of both hearing and balance. It is also, because of the delicacy of its construction and the vulnerability of its position on the body, highly prone to infection, injury and damage.

A chain of events involving bacteria in the ear can often be debilitating. Another look at the structure shows us that the brain cavity lies behind a thin plate of bone just above the middle ear. The nerve controlling the muscles of facial expression passes from the brain through the middle-ear cavity, then on through the mastoid bone, which is felt as a bump just behind the ear. That series of connections is especially susceptible to an acute middle-ear infection called acute otitis media. This inflammation of the inner ear may be caused by allergic reaction, a virus or bacteria – and there are likely to be complications. The inflammation can pass to the air cells in the mastoid bone, resulting in a dangerous mastoid abscess, which in turn raises the possibility of meningitis, facial nerve paralysis, septicaemia or a brain abscess.

Today, acute infections of that kind can usually be controlled by antibiotics. Life-threatening levels of disease of the ear and the mastoid air cells are found mainly in remote areas of the world where people are poorly nourished and have no access to adequate medical treatment. Which brings us back to the Greenland Vikings.

The visible thinning and erosion in the mastoid bones and other regions of the skull X-rays presented Dr Lynnerup with a clear backward glance: they showed him the condition of many people's health close to the time the Greenland Vikings disappeared. They had succumbed to middle-ear disease on a mounting scale. Decent food in reasonable quantities was probably not available, and so their resistance to infection was disastrously lowered.

Reduced quality of nutrition and deterioration of living conditions, coupled with Greenland's harsh climate, would have meant that more and more people would suffer from other common diseases such as pneumonia which, like middle ear infection, would have proved fatal to the weaker victims in the community.

As Dr Lynnerup continued his analysis of the bones, he discovered yet another important lead:

> We found that there was an over-representation of young, adult female skeletons in the graveyards, which could also indicate worsened living conditions, and we know that young females, along with infants and the very old, are those most susceptible to diseases.

BLOOD RED ROSES

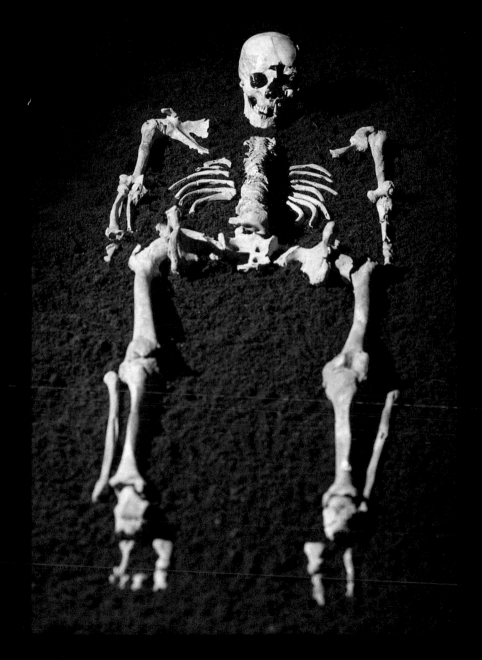

ABOVE • Remains of a soldier exhumed from the burial pit at Towton.

ABOVE • Medieval battlefield surgery lacked finesse but was surprisingly effective.

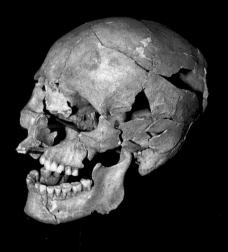

LEFT • The savagery of battle at Towton is evident from this victim's wounds.

CANYON CANNIBALS

TOP • The ruins of Pueblo Bonito, possibly the ceremonial centre of the Chaco world.

BELOW • Chetro Kettl, the largest of the Anasazi great houses.

LEFT • Templo Mayor, religious centre of a culture committed to human sacrifice.

RIGHT • Professor Christy Turner, key researcher into cannibalism in the American South-West.

LOST VIKINGS

BOTTOM LEFT • Mummy of an Inuit baby, about five hundred years old, exhumed by archaeologists in Greenland.

RIGHT • Remains of a bishop, buried with his symbols of office, unearthed near the Viking cathedral at Gardar.

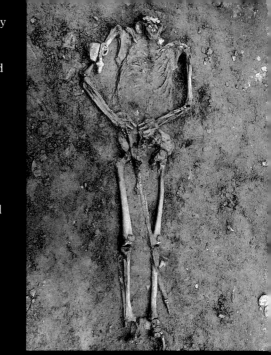

ABOVE • All that survives of a once prosperous Viking settlement

ABOVE • The church at Hvalsey, where Vikings burned a seducer at the stake.

BEWITCHED

ABOVE • The head of Grauballe man, an ergot victim who died approximately 2,000 years ago.

RIGHT • Rye infected with ergot. The dark elongated patch on the left

SYPHILIS ENGIMA

ABOVE • Treatments for syphilis; no course of action was too extreme in

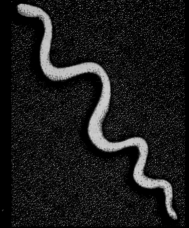

TOP LEFT • A hospital for lepers at Southwark, London.

TOP RIGHT • Electron micrograph of *Treponema pallidum*, the microbe that causes syphilis.

LEFT • Columbus, returning from his first voyage, enters Barcelona in triumph.

These discoveries certainly suggested a crisis. Young women of child-bearing age, the very people most important to the survival and growth of the settlements, had been dying off in disturbing numbers.

Dr Lynnerup's findings had a forerunner in an excavation carried out in 1921 by a Norwegian archaeologist at Herjolfsnes in southern Greenland. The remains he excavated, which disclosed some of the most complete examples of ordinary Europeans' dress in the Middle Ages, were analysed long before modern technology on dating and disease was available, and in any case they were in a bad state of preservation. Nevertheless, they presented eloquent testimony to F. C. C. Hansen when he examined them in 1924. His theory about the twenty-seven individuals gives us a clue about their health:

> The women especially were thus not only small of stature, but in addition to this a conspicuously large number of them are of a slight and feeble build; they are narrow across the shoulders, narrow-chested and in part narrow at the hips. Several show symptoms of rickets, deformity of the pelvis, scoliosis and great differences in the strength and size of the right and left lower extremities.
>
> The tall northern race has thus degenerated into small, slight and delicate women, and correspondingly slightly taller men, a striking example of the well-known effect of chronic undernourishment and hard conditions of life on a population, especially on the physical development and stature of the children and younger individuals, when the injurious influence extends to several generations.

Hansen's analysis concentrated on two adult females he called Herjolfsnes I and II:

In a small isolated population such as that of the Norse colonies in Greenland, rickets and the resulting pelvic contractions in the women would in the long run mean a serious danger to the population, since the outlook for the mother and child in pregnancy and birth would grow less favourable when even slighter degrees of pelvic contraction and deformity grew more common, and for such women the risk increased at each succeeding pregnancy and birth, both for the life of the child and the mother.

Even if a woman after a difficult first labour had at the risk of her own life brought a living child into the world, her prospects for successful delivery grew less and less for the second and third time, and when, in addition to this, no effective obstetric aid could be counted upon, and the sanitary conditions were bad, it will easily be perceived what a source of danger the frequently occurring pelvic deformities must become with regard to the perpetuation of the population and the life of its women.

In the ruins of a silted-over farmhouse at the site of their farmstead excavations, archaeologists found a sombre pointer to what happened to other settlers. The bones of a newborn calf and a Norwegian elkhound – the Viking hunting dog – were found lying in the kitchen. The bones were heavily knife-marked. Both animals had been killed and eaten. The investigators were aware that no Viking would have killed and eaten his hunting dog, which was a hugely valuable resource in itself, unless he and his family had been starving.

A study of fossilized flies provided impressive evidence that a famine swept Greenland in the last years of the Viking colony. Dr Peter Skidmore of the University of Sheffield carefully pieced the story together, using flies recovered from rooms at the farmhouse where the bones of the dog were found. 'Fossilized flies can tell us a very great deal,' he said. 'Some of the material from Greenland that I've examined has been in amazing condition.'

He pointed to the tiny remains of a number of blackened, desiccated-looking flies, neatly aligned in two rows in a Petri dish:

> I have a batch of specimens extracted from one particular room in the Norse dwelling. That species only bred in situations that were warm. It's what they call a thermophilous fly, and it breeds in decaying animal matter. The sort of situation that this fly would require would be found in a dark, warm room with plenty of droppings – precisely a description of the Norse living room in those days.

As he had expected, Dr Skidmore found warmth-loving flies on the floors of the farmhouse living room and bedroom. In the food larder, another kind of fly had thrived. This species favoured colder conditions and survived on a diet of meat.

But on the topmost layer of silt, formed in the final days of the Vikings' occupation, he came across something very different. The warmth-loving flies had gone, and the cold-loving flesh-eaters had migrated to the bedroom. Skidmore knew what that could suggest: the flies had moved there to feed on the settlers' dead bodies.

Hoping to uncover the root cause of the tragedy, the archaeologists working on the project contacted scientists working in Greenland's daunting interior – the territory held in the grip of year-long permafrost – on the Greenland Ice Sheet Project, or GISP II. This involves drilling down through the ice sheet with a hollow drill and extracting a core of ice. The core obtained reveals the history of changes in the earth's climate in that region over the past 250,000 years. As soon as the core was extracted, it was shipped in sections by frozen transportation to the University of New Hampshire in the United States. 'The thickness of the ice in the area where we conducted our study is about 3,000 metres,' said Dr Paul Mayewski, who led the GISP II project. 'In fact, it's exactly 3,056.4 metres, because we drilled right down to the bedrock.'

At the time when moisture condenses to fall as snow, the air temperature controls the amounts of oxygen and hydrogen that the snow contains. Scientists are able to reconstruct temperature variations for a particular period by studying the appropriate levels of oxygen and hydrogen of the ice cores. As Dr Mayewski explained:

> The ice core is a 5.2-inch-diameter core, and what's particularly remarkable is that within any layer we can recover fifty different measures or descriptions of what the environment is like. So we now have the best preserved record of frozen atmosphere for that one particular year.

The ice cores show that around the year 1000, when the Vikings first became settlers in Greenland, the climate was better than those familiar even with the Danish climate might have expected. 'There is evidence when the Viking colony was first established that the weather was actually rather good,' said Judith Jesch. 'There is even a thirteenth-century Norwegian text which says that the weather in Greenland, in the summer at any rate, was nicer than in either Iceland or Norway.'

But that state of affairs was not going to last. We now know that the climate got gradually colder. To find out just how cold it became, one scientist carried out an analysis of the atoms inside the ice cores. Dr Lisa Barlow of the University of Colorado was looking for deuterium. She explained:

> Most water molecules are made out of two hydrogen atoms and one oxygen atom. A very small percentage of water molecules are made out of one hydrogen and one heavy hydrogen – which is called deuterium – and an oxygen molecule. Now, these water molecules with the deuterium are slightly heavier, and so they respond differently to processes like evaporation and precipitation.

When the weather is warm, deuterium evaporates readily to become part of the atmosphere. When the atmospheric temperature drops to freezing, however, deuterium's relative heaviness impedes its evaporation. The result is that less of it falls later as a component of the snow. 'So if you have a profile from the surface of the snow,' said Dr Barlow, 'looking down through time, you have this nice seasonal signal where in the summertime there is a little bit more of the deuterium, in the wintertime there is a little less.'

Dr Barlow found that the sections of ice core from the end of the Greenland Vikings' time contained abnormally low quantities of deuterium. She concluded that the climate had grown considerably colder. In fact, when the ice-core examination was taken a stage further, it was revealed that a little ice age had swept over Greenland. Dr Mayewski expanded on this:

> When the Norse travelled to Greenland during the medieval warm period, the conditions were relatively

mild. Having lived there for many generations, they would have been extremely surprised to suddenly find out that things were changing around them.

But this evidence of the run of cold summers came only from the ice taken from the centre of Greenland. To find out if the climate also changed at the coastal settlements, Dr Henry Fricke of the University of Michigan compared the ice-core findings with evidence from the Vikings' bodily remains. He knew that an accurate record of the weather during their lifetime could be found in their teeth:

> In my research I'm taking this one step further, and I'm using the oxygen–isotope ratio of tooth enamel to act as a record or a proxy for that of local rain or snow. And we can do that because in the case of the Norse they were probably getting their drinking water from little ponds, streams or meltwater from snow. Water from the surface gets incorporated into their bodies, then into their blood and then eventually into their teeth, so that the oxygen–isotope ratio of their tooth enamel can act as a record of the temperature at the time that person was living.

Dr Fricke worked with teeth taken from Viking graveyards in various parts of coastal Greenland. He needed only a few grains from the surface of each tooth for his tests. He used a hand drill fitted with a dental burr to take a quantity from each in the form of powder. The samples then had to be scrupulously analysed one by one. The 650-year-old tooth enamel was first mixed with hydrofluoric acid, which caused it to dissolve. 'The goal of the technique,' said Fricke, 'is to get the oxygen out of the tooth enamel and into a form that we can analyse on our mass spectrometer.'

Silver nitrate solution was next added to the liquid, then the mixture was heated. This procedure created a rich yellow powder called silver phosphate. The silver phosphate, with a few added particles of graphite, was put into a strong heat-resistant cylinder. The cylinder was then sealed and flame-heated to 1,400° Celsius. The silver phosphate reacted with the graphite to form a gas – carbon dioxide. 'It's this carbon dioxide that we can then introduce into the mass spectrometer,' said Dr Fricke.

Mass spectrometry is an analytic technique that identifies substances by separating and counting their ions in a gas, using magnetic and electrical fields to effect the separation. It is one of the most sophisticated detection and identification techniques available to forensic science.

Fricke's test results confirmed a general drop in Greenland's surface temperature close to the middle of the fourteenth century. This coincided with the time when the emissary Ivar Bardarson found the western settlement deserted. 'This evidence confirms the results that the people working on ice cores produced,' said Dr Fricke. 'The cooling that they observed in those ice cores was in fact lived through by the people right there on the coast of Greenland.'

An ice age, even in miniature, would have devastated the Vikings' system of farming. Lisa Barlow believed it caused their hay crops to fail, which would have left the cattle and sheep without food for the winter. 'If you have lower summer temperatures, then that affects the amount of grass that can be grown. These people are trying to feed their cows for the next nine months of winter on whatever they can grow in the summertime.'

Proof that the harvest failed came from the University of Sheffield; specifically, it came from the fossilized beetles that had once lived in the fields and haylofts of Viking Greenland. When scientists at Sheffield counted these fossils, it was clear that their numbers had dwindled considerably in the final years of the settlements. This was a sign of crisis. The production of hay must have slumped, as one of the Sheffield team explained:

> In some of the later samples, changes in the fauna suggest that the hayfield is being denuded, that either they are so short of hay they are over-exploiting it or they are over-grazing it. And the reason they are taking too much hay is that they haven't enough to keep their animals alive through the winter. Eventually, you reach a critical point where you can't maintain your breeding population of animals, and if your stock dies, then you die.

After working on the lost Vikings case for more than forty years, Dr Bent Fredskild does not blame the disappearance of the Vikings entirely on the mini ice age. He maintains that the Vikings were having difficulty in raising fodder for their livestock long before the temperatures took a drop in the 1340s. During his many research visits to Greenland he took hundreds of mud cores from the beds of lakes. These, he found, contained samples of earth and peat blown off the meadows in Viking times. This indicated to him that the settlers had overgrazed the land, which in turn caused widespread erosion. Overgrazing in Greenland has been a problem in modern times, too. The animals have sometimes eaten away the ground cover that was previously thick with native plants like sedge, cotton grass and dwarf birch and willow. When the cover of vegetation is breached and broken up, the slicing winds coming over the inland ice sheet rip the soil apart and blow it away. Dr Fredskild is convinced that the Vikings turned their pastures into a wilderness simply by overgrazing.

It is easy enough to picture the plight of the Vikings and see how slender their chances of survival must have been. It is not difficult, either, to sympathize and to picture their growing despair in the teeth of relentless nature. Yet Greenland's other people, the Thule Inuit, survived that terrible time.

Maariu Olsen, an Inuit historian, elaborated: 'This land is big, it's beautiful,' he said, 'but it is also very harsh. You have to have certain skills to survive. This was especially true in the old days. The Vikings didn't really catch the meaning of life here.'

The Inuit, together with the closely related Aleut, form the greater part of the native population of the Arctic and sub-Arctic regions of Greenland, Alaska, Canada and Siberia. Their name varies from country to country, and depending on region they call themselves Inuit, Inupiat, Yupik or Alutiit, each of which is a variation of 'the people' or 'the real people'. The name Eskimo, applied to Arctic people by Europeans and others since the sixteenth century, is an Algonquian word once thought to mean 'eaters of raw flesh' but now believed to mean 'snowshoes'. The Arctic peoples of Canada and Greenland favour the name Inuit; in Alaska they still prefer to be called Eskimo.

The oldest known Inuit culture was on Umnak Island in the Aleutians: scientific dating of the site produced an age of 3,018, plus or minus 230 years. In the late twentieth century there were an estimated 117,000 Inuit in the world: 51,000 in Greenland and Denmark, 43,000 in Alaska, 21,000 in Canada and 1,600 in Siberia.

The Inuit are an Asian people and can be clearly distinguished from the Native Americans by their more Asian features and their relatively smaller hands and feet. Another feature that distinguishes the Inuit is the high incidence of type B blood in their populations, while the same blood type seems to be completely absent from Native Americans. Since blood type is a very stable characteristic of heredity, anthropologists believe that the Inuit population is, at least in part, different in origin from the Native Americans and that they are not, as was earlier believed, simply an Indian people who developed as a separate culture in the north. The Inuit-Aleut languages, so different in their structure from those of the Native Americans, are nevertheless close in structure to each other, even though there are a large number of worldwide variants.

Inuit civilization was wholly adapted to a cold, icebound environment and was the outcome of an inventive material culture, patient endurance and innate fatalism. They were also an economical people; practically every part of every animal they killed was put to use. Clothes were made from the skins of birds and animals, sewn with sinew thread and bone needles. They wore hooded jackets, trousers and boots, all made from leather lined with fur, and all waterproof. Hunters' highly protective over-clothes were waterproof, too, and made from the intestines of seals and walruses. Skins were also made into tents and boat covers.

There was never a substantial vegetable component in the Inuit diet. The staple foods were caribou, seal, walrus, whale meat, whale blubber and fish. Harpoons were used to kill seals, which were hunted on the ice or from one-man skin-covered canoes called kayaks. Whales were hunted with large boats called umiaks. Bows and arrows were used in summer to hunt caribou and any other wild animals that could be found. Dog sleds were the standard land transportation. Most Inuit wintered in snow-block houses – igloos – or semi-subterranean dwellings of cut sod heaped on frameworks made of whalebone or wood. It was common for the Inuit to spend the summer in animal-skin tents.

There were no tribes in traditional Inuit society. A group of people was known by a place name with the suffix 'miut', meaning 'people of'.

The primary unit of social organization was the extended family: a man, his wife, their unmarried children and their married sons and their wives and children. A number of family groups would often join forces and exploit an area's food resources.

Inuit religion was animistic, which means that they perceived the existence of the soul as something distinct from the body, and they firmly believed in a spiritual world, ascribing souls to animals and to all the major features of the environment, including wind and rain. 'So many souls,' a commentator wrote, 'and so many to be appeased for such myriad reasons.'

Prayers were said for the souls of animals killed for food; it was one thing to kill an animal, but quite another to do so callously or with disrespect. There was a tradition of an Inuit wife offering the courtesy of a drink of water to a dead seal when her husband brought it in from a day's hunting.

The central religious figure was the shaman, who had a number of serious duties. He had to discover the reason for poor hunting, which was often believed to result from a member of the family or the community of families breaking the taboos relating to food or hunting. The shaman was also required to diagnose illness and to treat it, and to serve as spiritual adviser and general comforter during bad times.

Inuit artistic impulses seem to have leaned mostly to dancing and the composing of songs. Being a very practical people, they expressed manual creativity through etched decorations on their ivory harpoon heads, decorated needle cases, elaborate stitching and small carvings from soapstone.

The Thule culture was a prehistoric Inuit culture that was developed along the Arctic coast of northern Alaska and probably as far to the east as the Amundsen Gulf. They spread eastwards rapidly, beginning around AD 900 and reaching Greenland by the twelfth century. They were hunter-gatherers by earliest tradition and today, in Greenland's least accessible areas, the Inuit still survive by hunting.

The Thule Inuits had not been settled in Greenland for as long as the Vikings, but they brought with them the kind of in built survival skills that the Vikings never possessed. A remarkable discovery shows how true this was. The mummified bodies of a group of Inuits were found recently, preserved in the Greenland permafrost. Carbon dating showed that they lived at approximately the same time that the Vikings ceased to be a presence in Greenland. Their clothing, tough and supremely functional against the vicious climate, protected them from the elements even in death. The discovery of the mummies soon brought scientists working on the mysterious disappearance of the Vikings closer to discovering why the Vikings' apparent mastery of their environment was so tragically reversed. Judith Jesch took up the tale:

> We can see that as conditions grew colder in Greenland,
> the Vikings didn't actually adapt very well to the change.
> At Herjolfsnes in the south of Greenland, archaeologists
> have found clothing from the fifteenth century. This is
> typical woollen clothing of the latest fashion. They wore
> hooded capes with long tails that were the height of
> fashion at that time. And that was fine, but it wasn't warm
> enough for the conditions that were prevalent in that
> period. The mummified bodies of the Inuit people were all
> dressed appropriately in furs and hides and were clearly
> much better adapted to survive this mini ice age.

One theory is that the mummified members of the Inuit family were passengers on a ship and perished in some accident at sea. On drifting to shore, their bodies were probably mummified by the dry winds. Their unusually fine state of preservation has enabled them to be studied with a thoroughness that is tantamount to luxury for the dedicated archaeologist and historian. They found all the outer clothes to be fastidiously stitched from well-cut skins of caribou or seals, the hide tough and thick enough to protect the wearer from dangerously low temperatures.

It was hard not to conclude that, when cold deepened and the relentless chill seeped to the Vikings' bones, they succumbed to a disaster they had wreaked on themselves. Like the victims of many an extinction before and since, they failed to adjust to the evolving demands of an environment undergoing massive change.

The Inuit adapted and survived, as they do on Greenland to this day. Down through the centuries their outlook has seen no variation, and acknowledging the superiority of nature has always been central to their way of life. During the mini ice age, the Inuit did not starve. However cold the weather, there would always have been prey to catch if the hunter had the appropriate skills. The historical record and the evidence of the middens suggest that the Viking settlers were not successful hunters; nor were they adroit at abandoning customs more suited to a kinder climate.

Professor Thomas McGovern, from New York's City University, who co-ordinated the investigation into the disappearance of the Vikings, commented as follows:

The Norse in Greenland certainly perished at a time of climatic change, a time where the changes were mostly unfavourable to them. But it is good to recognize that not everybody in Greenland perished at the same time. The Inuit, who by this point were living in most parts of Greenland, survived quite nicely as far as we know through the same period, and they were the ancestors of the Greenlandic population which exists today. So

Greenland did not become uninhabitable for all humans. In fact, some humans, these hunters, did fine throughout the same time period. What they *did* become, though, was extremely hostile to the kind of society the Norse Greenlanders had constructed. A society that had all these trappings of medieval Europe, the society that had its bishops, its monasteries, its nunneries, its rich men, its poor men. All the bits of medieval Europe which had come into Greenland at this point were expensive. They were expensive socially, and they were expensive environmentally as well.

A question that remained was whether the Vikings took up serious hunting and fishing as conditions changed or whether they simply carried on in their traditional ways, farming cattle and sheep in spite of the grim warnings being handed out by nature.

Animal bones from an archaeological dig at the Eastern Settlement produced evidence relevant to this question. The bones, together with each and every fragment discarded by the Vikings who occupied the farmstead, were gathered up, bagged, boxed and labelled. When the excavation finally closed, the investigators had accumulated 50,000 samples, ready to be sent for analysis and evaluation to centres of scientific excellence around the world.

A number of the bones ended up in the heart of New York at City University, adding to the prodigious archives of Professor McGovern. By studying the bones in conjunction with information about the various layers in which they were found, Professor McGovern could make informed deductions about the Greenland Vikings' diet and how it varied over time.

He described a collection of bones on a tray:

This is a pretty typical set of remains from this archaeological excavation. Some of these things are cattle bones
brought in from Europe. Here's a little piece of a sheep
jaw; goats, pigs, dogs, horses. Some of them, however, are
animals that are wild local animals like caribou, or other
animals like seals.

Professor McGovern's conclusion was that the Greenland Vikings
turned to fishing and hunting only when the mini ice age threatened their
food supplies. Even then, compared with their Viking neighbours in
Iceland, they ate very little food from the sea.

Professor McGovern introduced another trayful of bones, a comparable selection from Viking Iceland, deposited at the same time as the
bones from Greenland. 'We can see that there's again a bunch of bones,
but they're different. They're fish bones. We have some birds present, too,
and we have little fragments of whale bones, but most of this tray is fish,
including one great big ling – it got in there somehow. A lot of cod …'

A few seal bones found in Greenland suggest that the Vikings
attempted to acclimatize by adjusting their diet from what was scarce to
what was relatively plentiful, but the evidence suggests that they failed.

Fossils of *Sarcophaga carnaria* – the flesh fly, commonly known as the
blowfly – from Viking and Eskimo middens have persuaded entomologist
Dr Peter Skidmore that the Vikings went hungry while the Inuit had more
food than they could eat:

The species that indicate carrion in the midden are the
blowflies. It appears from the fly remains present that
there was no carrion or even marrow on the Norse
middens. We know that there was a lot of bone material,

but there was no marrow. In contrast, the Eskimo midden contained an enormous amount of carrion and masses of marrow. They had plenty of it. They were availing themselves of the seals and the fish in the fjords. The Norse economy seemed to have been based entirely on sheep and cattle. So they were taking all the marrow out of the bones, and they were scraping them clean and probably boiling all the meat off as well. The conclusion that one would be forced to draw from that would be that the Eskimos could be profligate with meat products.

One question was raised by that assessment: why didn't the Vikings learn to hunt from the Inuit? Professor McGovern proposed an answer:

The Church may have played a role in this strange barrier between these two cultures. You may think that the Norse and the Inuit actually did not coexist in Greenland at all, because there are so few finds of Inuit objects on Norse farms. And there are so few examples of Norse adaptation. Why would a Norse seal-hunter not pick up some of the Inuit technology? I think part of the answer is that if you went and talked to an old, experienced Inuit hunter and persuaded him to teach you a few secrets, he would have talked to you about how to give water to the seal when it is brought up to the ice, he would talk to you about the proper prayers to say as you were doing it.

From the standpoint of the Church, what the Inuit would be doing was filling the Viking's head with heathen mumbo-jumbo. It is not hard to imagine the Church putting limits on any association between the two cultures. 'There certainly was a barrier maintained between them,' Professor McGovern said. 'It wasn't accidental; it had to have been maintained at some considerable trouble and expense on somebody's part for a long period.'

Professor McGovern is convinced that the Church warned the Greenland Vikings that the Inuit should be avoided because they were heathens, and heathens were anathema. No good Christian at that time would have considered going against the will of the Church. If the priests and bishops decreed that Vikings and Inuit should have only the most cursory of contact, then the existing cultural gaps in Greenland would have immediately widened. If the Vikings were fearful of associating with their neighbours, they would never learn anything from them, even in a crisis.

The number of churches built in Greenland at the time of the settlements shows how dominant a position the Christian religon occupied in the lives of the Viking settlers. These churches formed the core both of the people's faith and their society. It was significant that the man called Kollgrim who apparently seduced a married woman was burned to death beside the church at Hvalsey.

From *Erik the Red's Saga* we learn that the conversion of the Greenlanders was achieved peacefully. Erik himself was the only person who showed any resistance when his son, Leif the Lucky, brought Christianity from Norway. The saga claims this came about on the initiative of the Norwegian king, Olaf Tryggvasson, shortly after the settlement in Greenland was established. Some historians have questioned the saga on this point. One of them, Ólafur Halldórsson, has suggested that the honour of having brought Christianity to Greenland fell to Norway's King Olaf Haraldsson, and that it happened in about 1012.

If we can trust the *Saga of Einar Sokkason*, the Greenlanders eventually got a bishop of their own about a hundred years later, at the beginning of the twelfth century. The story is thought to have been written by an anonymous author in around the year 1200 and goes as follows. At a communal meeting the Greenland farmers decided that they should share among them the expense of installing and paying partial support for a bishop. One of their number, Einar Sokkason, was sent to Norway to present the proposition to the king. The king considered it and finally complied with the Greenlanders' request; he appointed the Norwegian clergyman Arnald as Bishop of Greenland. After some negotiation between Arnald and the Greenland Vikings (no details of these are given in the saga), Arnald accepted the appointment. Three years later he sailed to Greenland and settled there, at Gardar in the Eastern Settlement. Interestingly, a grave unearthed in recent times in the precincts of the Viking cathedral at Gardar contained the bones of a bishop. The badges of office – the holy ring and the crosier – had been buried with him.

Evidence exists to show the scale of the Church's influence in Greenland. During the fourteenth century, apart from collecting tithes from the farms, the Church imposed an export tax that must have led to serious deterioration in the income from trade. Yet there is no record of any organized or even isolated protest. We also learn that the great bulk of the hunting rights in Greenland belonged to the Church. So although reindeer, polar bears and whales were plentiful, people could hunt these creatures only with the bishop's permission, and permission had a price attached. It is clear from the records that not only did the Church hold spiritual sway over the Greenland Vikings, but it also grew to become a suzerain, or feudal overlord. In time, the bishops and the Roman Church between them became the biggest landowners in Greenland.

Today the scientists are beginning to piece together the story of the downfall years of the Greenland Vikings. Their demise began with an abrupt change in the climate that brought an intensifying of bleak and arctic conditions. The miniature ice age that engulfed them brought crop failure and the consequent death of their livestock from starvation. Undernourished and cold, the people succumbed to pneumonia, ear, nose and throat infections, plus other severe and debilitating illnesses. Weakened by infection and malnutrition, the young women and children died. Late in the day their elders tried to adopt the hunting and fishing strategies of the Inuit, but they had no ingrained skills and none of the very stamina that enabled the Inuit to carry out the hard work of food-gathering. Desperate and bereft of alternatives, the settlers slaughtered their hunting dogs for food, one more step on the road to cancelling all hope of surviving in that fearsome and unyielding place. 'It seems to me very clear that they were living at the limit of possible sustained existence,' said Peter Skidmore. 'Had they gone over to the Inuit lifestyle of adapting more to their environment, they may have survived. But I think that they came to a situation where it was just not possible to continue their lifestyle.'

A number of loose ends remain, some crucial questions that the investigators have so far failed to answer, one of them posed by Professor McGovern:

> One thing that is puzzling from this whole grim story of the end of Norse Greenland is where are the human bones? That is the real question. We have virtually no human bones from inside Norse houses that are contemporary with the end of the settlement. They are just not there. We have plenty of people buried in the churchyard, but that is the sort of thing that happens in an orderly

society, in a society that is still functioning. What happened to the last ones? And the clear answer to this question is: we don't know.

Dr Judith Jesch put forward a suggestion: 'Personally, I think the most likely explanation is that the colony dwindled until they were very small in number and probably they sailed away and either never arrived or went somewhere else, and we don't know whereabouts that was.'

Many scientists infer from all the evidence, and from the brief catalogue of what was likely, that sheer adversity drove the settlers in the Western Settlement to find refuge on warmer, more congenial shores. They may have tried to go back to Scandinavia, which their ancestors had left 500 years before. There have been suggestions that they tried to sail to America. But wild and treacherous seas lay between them and whatever destination they may have tried to reach. Professor McGovern reached his own conclusion:

> My own speculation to throw into the pot is that, well, if you were failing in your farm and your whole settlement was going down, a last resort might be to get into your boat and try to go to the Eastern Settlement. And Greenland, as everyone who has sailed there can attest, is a dangerous place. And just because you set out on a journey doesn't mean you make it. So one location for the last of the Norse Greenlanders may simply be at the bottom of the sea.

4

BEWITCHED

THERE IS AN OLD AND worldwide belief that certain people, most of them women, can exercise supernatural powers for purposes of evil. The witch as a concept has been around probably since human beings followed their grouping instinct and formed communities. In literature, witchcraft is mentioned as far back as Homer; it was a witch, Medea, who helped Jason retrieve the golden fleece from Colchis. The Roman poet Horace – full name Quintus Horatius Flaccus, who lived from 65 to 8 BC – gave a very detailed description of the behaviour of a couple of witches in the Esquiline cemetery. The Bible has several references to witchcraft, a notable one being when King Saul, failing to communicate with God, decided instead to consult a witch:

> Then said Saul unto his servants, Seek me a woman that
> hath a familiar spirit, that I may go to her, and enquire of
> her. And his servants said to him, Behold, there is a woman

that hath a familiar spirit at Endor. And Saul disguised
himself, and put on other raiment, and he went, and two
men with him, and they came to the woman by night: and
he said, I pray thee, divine unto me by the familiar spirit,
and bring me him up, whom I shall name unto thee
(I Samuel 28: 7, 8).

The early Church authorities took the official view that witchcraft
was without power and that it relied wholly for its effect on a talent for
deception exercised by certain manipulative women; simple utterance of
the name of Jesus Christ was enough to turn aside the deceivers and
neutralize their wiles. This approach was reinforced by repeated sermons
condemning the practice of witchcraft.

But condemnation often stirs curiosity. Belief in witchcraft
spread, probably encouraged by the Church's warnings against it,
which put ideas into the heads of unsophisticated people who had
heard neither of the dark arts nor of the intriguing possibilities of
supernatural powers. The link between Satan and witchcraft gained
emphasis with the rise of the dualist doctrine, which invested the devil
with awesome potency as God's equally matched adversary. Satan was the
supreme spirit of evil, the tempter and spiritual enemy of mankind.
He was dark and he embodied power; dark power suited the image
of the witch, and as soon as witchcraft was thought to involve
traffic with demons, it came within the remit of the Inquisition. Witches
were now fair game.

Throughout Europe between the late Middle Ages and the early
eighteenth century, fervent opposition to the 'loathsome harpies', as a
contemporay broadsheet described them, took on the proportions of a
popular sport. There were public trials, many of which ended with

executions that were motivated by a clear biblical directive: 'Thou shalt not suffer a witch to live' (Exodus 22: 18).

In medieval times, perhaps more so than at any other period of history, popular belief in witches as the true handmaidens of Satan was widespread and deeply embedded. Night-time was their cover, and the night was when they were hunted. In Shakespeare's time, the sense of lurking, putrid evil was intensely real:

> 'Tis now the very witching time of night,
> When churchyards yawn and hell itself breathes out
> Contagion to this world: now could I drink hot blood,
> And do such bitter business as the day
> Would quake to look on (*Hamlet* III, ii).

Witches caused harm, and they could do so from a distance. Young girls went into trances or became hysterical for reasons that neither they nor physicians could understand. Babies failed to thrive. Objects kept changing their position in rooms every time certain old persons' backs were turned until they were driven demented. Domestic animals attacked their owners. It was all clearly witchcraft, and worrying questions arose every time a household or a community showed signs of having attracted the malice of someone in league with Satan. Who in the community practised witchcraft? Why was this happening here, when a couple of kilometres away people lived in peaceful, undiluted Christian harmony untroubled by evil?

The second question taxed many a scribe and cleric of the Middle Ages. Witchcraft was always sporadic, never epidemic. If the devil and his cohorts were as potent in their way as God himself, why didn't they cover the globe in their darkness? Why not bedevil a continent at a time, or at least an entire country? Did the dark ones choose not to? If so, why? Was it for arcane, frightful reasons that no human could understand? Or was it the case, as some claimed, that in profoundly godly communities and in households without taint, the devil and his kind could not penetrate the natural barrier erected by virtue? The question of witchcraft's intermittent nature only raised more questions.

Now, centuries later, scientific research has hit upon a possible explanation for 'bewitchment'. The very same research has uncovered a fascinating link between the widespread acid-tripping cult of the 1960s and what was once medieval Europe's staple diet. And the line of discovery does not stop there. The new hypothesis might just have solved a long-standing puzzle from Europe's past.

The first clue to the mysteries of sporadic witchcraft and demonic possession is 3,000 years old. Peat-cutters working in the Danish village of Grauballe in 1951 came across the buried and perfectly preserved body of an adult male, later estimated to have died in the Neolithic Period. The corpse was removed to an examination room, where it was noticed that the dead man's throat had been cut from ear to ear; this is suspected to have been a ritualistic form of killing.

The body was opened and the stomach contents removed. On examination, these were found to contain a large number of partly digested ears of a cereal crop, very obviously blighted with a dark mould. This proved, on testing, to be ergot, a naturally occurring substance that is highly toxic and hallucinogenic.

Technically speaking, ergot is a fungus (its Latin name is *Claviceps purpurea*) that affects the ripe grains of certain cereals, particularly rye. The spores of ergot lie dormant in the soil all through the winter. When the young plants begin to grow, they take up the spores, and if the weather conditions work out favourably the ergot begins a new life cycle. One by one, the ears of grain are replaced by black, spur-like prominences. These can be highly poisonous. In a bad year, a harvest will yield as much ergot as grain.

Ergot is a true ecbolic – which means it is capable of expelling the foetus from a pregnant uterus. Among its actively poisonous constituents are the chemicals ergotoxine, ergotamine and ergometrine. Under controlled conditions, ergot is a neat concentrate of substances that can be separately extracted in the laboratory or manufacturing plant.

Ergotoxine causes contraction of the womb at the end of pregnancy in human females, though it has very little effect during the time the baby is coming to term. A rather more alarming feature of ergotoxine is that by contracting the arterioles – tiny arteries that hook up with the body's capillary network – it eventually causes gangrene. Ergotoxine is in fact the most important factor in ergot poisoning. The second chemical ergotamine is very similar to ergotoxine.

Ergometrine is the component mainly responsible for the action of ergot on the womb. Within a few minutes of being administered, it brings on prolonged muscular contraction of the uterine muscle, which is especially sensitive following the delivery of a baby. That makes ergometrine very useful for controlling the haemorrhage that occasionally follows the expulsion of the afterbirth. It differs from the other chemical constituents of ergot by being less active in the process of causing gangrene.

There is a reported case, from the 1950s, of a woman of thirty who became pregnant and did not want to have the child. From an illicit vendor she bought a twelve-ounce (340-gramme) bottle of liquid which she was told contained ergot; at that time the chemical extract had an undeserved reputation as a safe abortion agent. The woman drank the bottle over a period of a week, but nothing happened. She bought a stronger mixture from the same person and was told she should spread the doses over a seven-day period, as previously. However, before the bottle was finished her arms began to ache terribly. Next, her skin started to itch, then her fingers swelled up. Her left index finger became very cold and turned dark blue at the tip. Fairly rapidly the remaining fingers on both hands were affected; later, four of them turned gangrenous as far as the end joints. The foetus was not aborted.

In hospitals today, commercially produced ergometrine is given to mothers by intramuscular injection for the routine management of the third stage of labour after the baby's shoulders have been delivered, thus aiding in the remainder of the delivery by causing the womb to contract. For high-risk cases of postpartum (after-childbirth) haemorrhage, the drug is given intravenously.

Only a few fatal cases from acute ergot poisoning have been recorded, and then only when very large quantities of the drug have been taken. The symptoms of acute poisoning are pain in the stomach, nausea, vomiting (with or without bleeding), a weak, rapid pulse, a feeling of pressure in the chest, coldness of the body, muscular cramps, lessening of sensation, gangrene in the toes and fingers, convulsive jerking, stupor, delirium, convulsions and coma.

The symptoms of chronic poisoning are gastrointestinal irritation, nervous exhaustion or excitement that sometimes amounts to mania, and a dry, waxen gangrene of the fingers and toes. When ergot actually kills someone, the autopsy shows profuse leakage of blood from ruptured vessels into the stomach, liver, kidneys and the abdominal cavity, together with evidence of gangrene of the fingers and toes.

Depending on the strain of the ergot he consumed, Grauballe Man would have died while suffering either shuddering convulsions or rapidly developing gangrene, or perhaps both. His disturbing symptoms could have been terrifying to a community unable to interpret them, and that raises an intriguing question: was Grauballe Man killed because of his bizarre behaviour and weirdly changing appearance? Primitive communities executed their neighbours for less.

How does ergot figure in witchcraft and demonic possession? To find out, we have to go a stage further with the ergot story. While investigating the possibilities for extended use of ergot in obstetrics, a Swiss scientist, Albert Hoffman, discovered that the fungus also had hallucinogenic properties. The story goes that he accidentally spilled some drops of a solution of ergot on his hand and licked it off. Minutes later he began to experience the most vivid and bizarre hallucinations. He had in fact stumbled on to the drug that would eventually be called Lysergic Acid Diethylamide – more familiarly, LSD.

By 1976 LSD was well known and in fairly regular use, even though it was not an approved drug. At that time Linnda Caporael, a psychologist, was preparing a paper for a history class; her thesis was that, historically, women had been every bit as evil as men. As an example she cited Ann Putnam, one of the principal witnesses in the 1692 witch trials in Salem, Massachusetts. Ann had claimed that another member of the community was a witch and that she had caused Ann and others to be possessed by the devil. Ann's story was backed and embellished by the other girls. They were able collectively to convince a court that their fits, their outbreaks of obscene babbling and their orgiastic behaviour in the woodland on the edge of Salem village, close to the town of Salem, were the work of witchcraft, performed by local women and men who had submitted to possession by Satan. At the time of the outbreak of strange behaviour among the girls, animals had been displaying disturbing signs too. Among cattle and swine there had been isolated fits and a spate of spontaneous abortions, oddities that appeared to support the notion of witches' mischief. The evidence put forward by Ann Putnam and her young friends sent nineteen innocent people to the gallows.

Spite or jealousy have been common explanations put forward to explain why people have accused other people of witchcraft. But historians found it hard to accept such a straightforward explanation when they examined the facts of the Salem witch trials. As Winfield S. Nevins wrote in 1916 in his book *Witchcraft in Salem Village*:

> I must confess to a measure of doubt as to the moving causes in this terrible tragedy. It seems impossible to believe a tithe of the statements which were made at the trials. And yet it is equally difficult to say that nine out of every ten of the men, women and children who testified upon their oaths, intentionally and willfully falsified. Nor does it seem possible that they did, or could invent all these marvelous tales; fictions rivaling the imaginative genius of Haggard or Jules Verne.

Nor could Linnda Caporael believe that simple spite or jealousy had much to do with the tragedy of Salem. She believed that while only a combination of causes would account for the people's extraordinary behaviour, no group of explanations would be adequate without a believable reason why the 'afflicted' girls behaved in the way they did. To understand her approach to the task of solving the enigma, it is necessary to look at the background.

Towards the end of December 1691, in Salem village in Massachusetts, eight girls suffered sudden, mysterious 'distempers'. Two of the girls affected, Betty Parris and Abigail Williams, were the daughter and niece of the Reverend Samuel Parris, the local minister. They were seized with 'blasphemous screaming', intermittent trance-like states, convulsive seizures, odd static postures and wild gesturing with their arms. Physicians examined all the affected girls but could find no explanation for their eccentric behaviour.

In mid-February 1692, as the seizures continued and doctors still failed to determine a physical cause, one of them concluded that the girls had fallen under the influence of Satan. Samuel Parris conducted prayer services and organized community fasting in the hope of neutralizing the evil forces that contaminated their community. In an effort to expose the 'witches', a near neighbour of Parris, Mary Sibley, proposed an old English recipe for detecting the witch or witches in their midst: she persuaded a man called John Indian, the husband of Parris's Carib Indian slave Tituba, to bake a rye cake using the urine of the young victims to moisten the flour. This was counter-magic; any evil symptom could be cancelled or at least made vulnerable to cure by taking counter-measures that very often involved the use of the afflicted parties' urine. This was probably an extension of the common practice of diagnosing everything from urine, which was believed by some to carry the secret of everything that ailed a person, be it physically or mentally.

In the end John's wife Tituba baked the cake, which was eventually fed to the Reverend Parris's dog. If the dog behaved oddly after it ate the cake, then a case of infestation by a witch or witches would be proved. There is no record of what happened to the dog, if anything, but on that same day Samuel Parris, after long procrastination, suddenly made the first formal accusation of witchcraft.

Being under pressure to reveal the source of their illness, the girls named three local women. On 29 February 1692 warrants were issued for the arrests of Tituba and two old women generally disliked by people in the village, Sarah Good and Sarah Osborne. Osborne and Good insisted they were innocent of the accusations, but Tituba said that the devil appeared to her 'sometimes like a hog and sometimes like a great dog'. Tituba testified, furthermore, that a conspiracy of witches was at work in Salem.

The afflictions continued. On 1 March the local magistrates John Hathorne and Jonathan Corwin questioned Tituba, Sarah Good and Sarah Osborne in the meeting house in Salem. That day only Tituba confessed to witchcraft.

Over the next weeks, various townspeople approached the court and testified that they, too, had been harmed in unnatural ways by certain other residents of the village, or had seen strange apparitions of the same people. The witch-hunt gathered force, and many more people were accused.

Women whose behaviour or circumstances were in any way upsetting to the traditions or conventions of the community were regularly denounced. A number of those accused had records of crime – among them witchcraft – while others were practising Christians and steady churchgoers who, until that time, had enjoyed some prestige in the community.

On 11 April the examinations were transferred from the outlying farming region to the town of Salem. They were conducted by Deputy Governor Thomas Danforth and six of the colony's senior magistrates, among them Samuel Sewall. This council did not, however, have the authority to sit in judgement on accused witches, because the colony was still without a legal government. When the new governor, Sir William Phips, eventually came from England bearing the charter that established the government of Massachusetts Bay Colony, the jails – even those 24 kilometres away in Boston – were crammed with prisoners from Salem waiting for trial. Phips appointed a special Court of Oyer and Terminer ('Hear and Determine'), which first sat on 2 June to hear the case against one Bridget Bishop. She was found guilty of witchcraft, and on 10 June she was hanged.

Prior to the court's next sitting, Cotton Mather, a prominent Congregational minister and author, wrote to the court on behalf of himself and the other Boston clergy, recommending 'critical and exquisite caution', and wishing that 'there may be as little as possible of such noise, company and openness as may too hastily expose them that are examined'. The ministers also advised that spectral evidence (the alleged apparition of an accused person being seen by an accuser) and the test of touch (the abrupt ceasing of a convulsion when the sufferer was touched by an accused person) could not be accepted as proofs of witchcraft.

The court appeared largely to ignore the ministers' advice. The trials went on, and people continued to be put to death. The girls whose accusations had set the whole train of events in motion were present throughout the examinations and trials, appearing to be as badly afflicted as ever, babbling and screeching and causing such a commotion that the trials frequently had to be stopped until they could be calmed.

By September the jails were full: nearly two hundred people accused of witchcraft awaited disposition of their cases. On 9 September six people were tried and condemned; the same verdict was handed down on 17 September to a further nine defendants.

On 19 September Giles Corey was 'pressed to death' for refusing to stand trial. On 22 September Martha Corey, Margaret Scott, Mary Easty, Alice Parker, Ann Pudeator, Wilmott Redd, Samuel Wardwell and Mary Parker were all hanged. By now twenty people had been executed — nineteen hanged, one man 'pressed to death'. All the convictions had been obtained on the basis of spectral evidence and the test of touch. Those who died had consistently sworn they were not guilty. 'I am no witch!' cried Bridget Bishop, the first one to die. 'I am innocent. I know nothing of it.' No one who confessed to witchcraft was executed. From almost the start of the examinations it had been clear that those who confessed would not be put to death.

On 17 September 1692 the witchcraft trials at the Court of Oyer and Terminer were adjourned until 2 November, but in fact the court never again tried anyone on a charge of witchcraft. The Superior Court of Judicature, composed of the same magistrates who sat on the Court of Oyer and Terminer, met in January 1693. Of fifty indictments for witchcraft put before them by the grand jury, twenty cases came to trial. Three of the accused were condemned but were never executed; all the others were acquitted. In May Governor William Phips declared a general reprieve. The witchcraft frenzy was over.

On the track of a cause for the 'possession' of those eight girls at Salem, Linnda Caporael set out to check the facts for herself and to weigh the explanations that had already been put forward.

Modern accounts of the origins of the Salem witchcraft begin with Samuel Parris's Carib slave girl, Tituba. The traditional history ascribed to her is that she taught magic tricks to the daughter and niece of the minister, Betty Parris and Abigail Williams, and to several other girls of the village, and that during secret meetings in the parsonage kitchen she taught them diabolical incantations. The girls' subsequent bizarre behaviour was a direct outcome of these forays into the occult.

The basis for the story, Caporael found, was twofold. In 1702 John Hale, a minister from Beverly in Massachusetts, published a caution against divination in which he said he had been told that one of the 'distempered' girls from Salem had tried to see the future using an egg and glass, and she had afterwards suffered a 'diabolical molestation' and died. Using an egg in a glass as a symbolic crystal ball is an old English technique of divination. Hale did not say that Tituba was present when the experiment took place, or, for that matter, that more than one girl was involved. Caporael tried in vain to find any reference to an afflicted girl dying before Hale's publication date.

The other prop for the tradition of implicating the slave as the cause of it all, Caporael believes, is the simple fact that Tituba was from the Caribbean. Part of Puritan belief was that Native Americans worshipped the devil, who was frequently spoken of as a black man. It was odd that at her examination, Tituba was never asked about her experiences of witchcraft at her place of birth. The story that she infested the girls with her devilry seems to have sprung from the groundless assumption that Tituba, being a Carib, must have been acquainted with the black arts.

Having found Tituba an unlikely originator of the eight girls' afflictions, Caporael turned her attention to current interpretations of what was wrong. After the discussion of origins, she discovered, numerous diagnoses of the girls' behaviour diverge. The opinion most frequently accepted is that the girls' startling behaviour was fraudulent. They may have committed the deceit for purposes of scandal, or to escape punishment from their elders when rumours started to spread about their excursions into magic. M. L. Starkey, author of *The Devil in Massachusetts*, wrote that some of the girls 'were no more seriously possessed than a pack of bobby-soxers on the loose'. The main barrier to Caporael agreeing with the explanation of what she calls 'purposeful fraud' is the undoubted gravity of the girls' symptoms: every eyewitness agreed about the seriousness of the affliction.

C. W. Upham, writing in *Salem Witchcraft*, published in 1867, appeared to believe the descriptions and suggested that the girls were skilled at theatrical conjuration. He further suggested that they were talented ventriloquists and gifted actresses who, by 'long practice', were able to 'bring the blood to the face, and send it back again'. Upham assumed the girls learned these skills, and more, from Tituba. But there is no evidence that Tituba had any working knowledge of acting, ventriloquism, blood control or anything else requiring innate skill and patient study. On the available evidence, most of the people of Massachusetts, except for a number of the accused and their supporters, do not seem to have thought the girls were pretending. When the trials were over and the dust had settled, it was the general view of the citizens of New England that the girls had suffered demonic possession.

The next current interpretation Caporael had to consider was hysteria. The word has been bandied about freely and with varying degrees of misuse in recent years, and when it is proposed as an explanation of what happened at Salem, the accounts invariably start with Tituba teaching the girls magic in the minister's kitchen. In *The Devil in Massachusetts* Starkey uses the term loosely: the girls were hysterical, which is to say overexcited, and they executed a spectacular fraud on a community that thereafter succumbed to 'mass hysteria'. C. Hansen, in *Witchcraft at Salem*, enlists hysteria in a more clinical sense to connote mental illness. He asserts that witchcraft really was being practised in Salem; he believes that several of the people hanged were practising witches. The symptoms displayed by the girls, he goes on, had a psychological cause, promoted by their guilt over practising fortune-telling during their clandestine sessions with Tituba. Hansen says the mental sickness was contagious and that the witnesses and a majority of those who confessed to consorting with the devil had turned hysterical as a result of their terror of witchcraft. However, Caporael points out that if the girls did develop genuine hysteria, then all eight of them must have developed it simultaneously, which is distinctly hard to believe. There was also no precedent: previous charges of witchcraft levelled at other Puritan populations in New England had never induced mass hysteria.

Now Caporael turned to the third and final of the contemporary explanations – physiology. The possibility that the girls might have suffered a bodily ailment has scarcely ever been raised by commentators. In the beginning, though, the villagers did suggest that there might be a physical cause, and prior to any charges of witchcraft being made the Reverend Parris summoned the help of several physicians. In *The History of the Colony and Province of Massachusetts Bay*, published in 1936, Thomas Hutchinson wrote: 'there are a great number of persons who are willing to suppose the accusers to have been under bodily disorders which affected their imagination.' There is also a report of a journalist suggesting that Tituba had dosed the girls with a tincture of a semi-toxic herb; this was *Datura stramonium*, also known as the thorn apple but commonly called jimson weed (after Jamestown in Virginia). An account by a military diarist, writing in 1687, says: 'Several of the Soldiers went to gather a Sallad ... and lighting in great Quantities on an Herb called James-town-weed, they gathered it; and by eating thereof in plenty, were rendered apish and foolish.'

There has been room for research in this direction, but it would seem that because doctors of the time failed to diagnose a physical cause for the girls' condition, later historians tackling the Salem enigma did not pursue the possibility.

Linnda Caporael was reading and rereading everything she could find about the Salem trials, and now she was on a new tack, approaching the mystery with the growing conviction that some physiological malfunction had made the girls at Salem behave the way they did. The seriousness of their symptoms was underscored by a memoir written by Thomas Putnam, who had been the first citizen to go to Salem and file a complaint of witchcraft with the magistrates. He had three afflicted children in his house, and of his baby daughter he wrote:

> Our child which died about the middle of April 1692 was
> as well and as thriving a child as most was: till it was about
> eight weeks old ... Mary Estick and Sarah Cloyes and I

myself was taken with strange kinds of fitts: but it pleased Allmighty God to deliver me from them: but quickly after this our poor young child was taken about midnight with strange and violent fitts: it continewed two day and two night and then departed this life by a cruell and violent death being enuf to pierce a stony hart. It was near five hours a dying.

One night Caporael was rereading Winfield Nevins's *Witchcraft in Salem Village*, in which the author noted that he was 'at a loss to explain the hallucinations'. As Caporael said:

> That word, at that moment, just hit the spark. I had heard of ergot poisoning and knew that somehow LSD came from ergot. A friend had *Cooper's Pharmaceutical* on hand, and we looked up the symptoms of ergot and I just about fell over. It wasn't just the hallucinations but the form of the convulsions and pin-pricking, really distinctive symptoms reported for ergot and in the trial records.

Now she needed to find out how LSD was derived from ergot. She learned that the manufacturing process synthesized most of the toxic components of ergot, and that LSD produces its well-documented deviations from normal behaviour by blocking the action of serotonin, a chemical that transmits nerve impulses in the brain and is active in neural mechanisms important to sleep and sensory perception. She read Hoffman's description of his experiences when he experimented with the ergot fungus, comparing his recollections with the testimony of a Salem villager who reported seeing about a dozen strange objects appear in his chimney in a darkened room. 'He said they appeared to be like jelly and shivered and shook with an upward motion,' Caporael said. 'His wife saw nothing. The testimony is strongly reminiscent of the undulating lights and objects reported in LSD-induced experiences.'

Caporael was excited by the new and promising direction her research was taking. Thus far, though, all she possessed was a hypothesis. There was no hard evidence of ergotized rye having created the Salem girls' symptoms, and even if Caporael had a compelling explanation for the hallucinations, she had found nothing that would explain convulsive fits, erratic movements and the other strange manifestations reported in the trial records.

She continued to acquire and absorb as much research material as she could on the subject of ergot. Eventually, she came across a report of a terrible episode in a small French town in 1951.

On the evening of 27 August 1951, at Pont-St-Esprit in Provence, an arm of the statue of the Virgin Mary above the church fell to earth with a crash. The following morning, however, seemed like any other. The baker's daily batch of fresh rye flour was delivered early, as usual, although on that particular morning something was different. The flour had an odd greyish look about it; when it was made into dough it felt slimy and smelled very bad. The only way the baker could make his bread rise was to add a substantial batch of older flour to the dough mixture. Later in the morning the baker's customers queued for their bread as usual. Then, as the hours passed, the townspeople who had eaten the bread began to fall ill. Many of them suffered intense convulsions, and their hands and feet turned blue. By evening, the ones most seriously affected had begun to die. Later, it was discovered that the cause of the outbreak was ergot poisoning from the flour.

The convulsions described in that story had some close parallels to the behaviour reported among the afflicted girls at Salem. Also, a detail of the French story resonated curiously with the episode of the rye 'witch cake' being fed to the Reverend Parris's dog. A dog at Pont-St-Esprit, after eating the ergotized bread, had run around in wild, frantic circles and then chewed a rock until its teeth were all smashed. It then dragged its hind legs behind it for a while, before lieing down to die. If the witch cake eaten by Parris's dog had contained ergot, and if the dog had reacted in the same way as the French dog, it is easy to understand how compelling the witch-cake evidence would have seemed in seventeenth-century New England.

Suggesting that convulsive ergot poisoning was an activating element in Salem's outbreak of witchcraft would be one thing, but it would be quite another to put together substantial data to show it was more than just a possibility. Details of growing conditions, the chronology of events in Salem and the sequence and nature of symptoms would have to mesh if a reasonable case were going to be made. The picture to emerge should be one of a community smitten with an explicable systemic disorder affecting their bodies *and* their minds.

Sure now of her investigative route, Caporael set about discovering if evidence for ergotism (poisoning from eating ergotized grain) existed in Salem in 1692.

She began with a study of growing conditions. Wild rye is – and was – the most commonly found grass along the North American coast from Virginia to Newfoundland. It is also the most receptive host for ergot. Early colonists reportedly did not like to use it as cattle forage: it often made the cows sick with unspecified diseases. It was fair to presume, Caporael decided, that ergot existed in the New World before the arrival of the Puritans.

Rye was undoubtedly the most reliable grain in that part of the world and was well established by the 1640s. Freezing winters made autumn sowing hazardous, so spring sowing was standard. The rye seeded in April and harvest time was in August, but grain was stored in barns where it often lay for months before being threshed during the colder weather. Caporael found that the timing of events in Salem in 1692 matched that cycle. Threshing took place shortly before Thanksgiving (the fourth Thursday of November), the only holiday observed by the Puritans. The girls' symptoms began in December 1691. Late the following autumn, the witchcraft episode ended sharply; there is no record of the girls or anyone else in Salem being further afflicted.

All rye was probably infected with ergot to some extent. What determines the potential for ergotism is the extent of infection and the period of time over which the ergot is eaten, rather than the simple existence of ergot itself. In a letter written from New York in 1807, one doctor tells another: 'On examining a granary where rye is stored, you will be able to procure a sufficient quantity [of ergot-bearing husks] from among that grain.' Even by the time the letter was written, agriculture had not reached the point where methods had been devised for the extensive use of treatments for eliminating fungi. Caporael believes it is probable that the summer rye crop in 1691 was fairly light, since not everyone showed symptoms, not even entire household groups.

Certain weather conditions – warm, wet springs and summers – boost fungus infestation. The weather pattern for the years 1691 and 1692 can be gathered from comments in diaries of the time. In 1691 there was rain and high temperatures in spring, followed by a hot, stormy summer. The following year was a drought year, so ergot on the grain in 1692 would have been highly unlikely.

Now Caporael took a look at localization. The medical correspondent quoted above went on to say that 'Rye which grows in low, wet ground yields [ergot] in greatest abundance'. One of the loudest and most unruly of the afflicted children was Ann Putnam, the twelve-year-old daughter of

Thomas Putnam. Ann's mother also showed signs of being affected; Caporael notes that psychological historians have accused the senior Ann of trying to dispel her own neurotic ills through her daughter. Two other afflicted girls also lived in the Putnam house.

Thomas Putnam had inherited one of the village's largest holdings of land. A study of his father's will showed that a large part of the land, to the west of the village, was highly prized swampy meadows, which made good farmland. So the Putnam farm, and perhaps the whole western acreage of Salem village, may have been an area where contamination occurred readily. This is supported by the residential pattern of the accusers, the accused and those defending the accused living within the boundaries of Salem village. Apart from the afflicted girls themselves, thirty of thirty-two adult accusers lived in the west of the village; twelve of the fourteen accused witches lived on the east side, as did twenty-four of the twenty-nine defenders. The general residential pattern, combined with the factional tendencies of the eastern and western sides, played their part in the development of the witchcraft crisis.

The first girls to be afflicted showed a slightly different residential pattern. Careful study by Caporael revealed convincing explanations for infection in six of the eight victims.

Three of them lived in the Putnam residence, and if that were the source of the ergot, their exposure to the risk of ergotism would be obvious. The daughter and niece of Samuel Parris lived with him in the parsonage. That dwelling stood almost exactly in the centre of the village, but the girls' exposure to contaminated grain from western land can be explained. Two-thirds of Parris's salary was paid in kind – in his case, in provisions; the villagers contributed to his upkeep in proportion to their landholding. Since Putnam had a large landholding, and since he was a vigorous supporter of Parris in the minister's disagreement with the community, it is safe to assume there would be a substantial quantity of ergotized grain in the Reverend Parris's larder.

The three remaining girls lived to the east and outside the village boundaries. One of them, Elizabeth Hubbard, was a domestic servant of Dr Griggs. It is believable that the doctor, like the Reverend Parris, used Putnam's grain; Griggs was, after all, a professional man, not a farmer. He was the only doctor in town, so he probably treated the senior Ann Putnam, a woman known for her poor health, many times. Griggs may have traded his services for food, or he may have bought it from the Putnams.

Sarah Churchill, the seventh afflicted girl, was a domestic servant to a prosperous farmer whose farm was situated by the Wooleston River and could have provided good conditions for the invasion of ergot. To Caporael, though, it seemed more likely that Sarah Churchill's affliction was a fraud. It was May before she became involved in the witchcraft persecutions, several months after the other girls. She testified in only two of the cases, the first one being against her master. One person who gave evidence claimed that Sarah had admitted later to lying about herself and others.

How the remaining afflicted girl could have come into contact with ergotized grain is a mystery, says Caporael. The girl was Mary Warren, a servant in the Proctor household. Proctor had a big farm to the south-east of Salem; he would have had no need to buy food or trade for it. Both Proctor and his wife stood accused of witchcraft and were condemned by the court. None of the Proctor children showed any sign of being afflicted – in fact, three of them were accused and put in prison. A document produced as evidence against Proctor shows that Mary stayed in the village overnight. With whom she stayed, or how often, is not recorded.

Mary Warren played a curious part in the trials. She began as one of the afflicted, then she recovered and was accused of witchcraft by the seven other girls, and finally she became afflicted again. There are strong indications that at least her first bout of affliction could have been genuine ergotism. Four witnesses affirmed that Mary believed she had been 'distempered', and during her affliction she had thought she saw several apparitions. But when Mary recovered and was behaving rationally, she did not recollect seeing any phantoms. Caporael has suggested that Mary's apparent second affliction may have been the outcome of intense pressure experienced during her examination by the magistrates.

In the published account of her researches, under the heading 'Ergotism and the Testimony', Linnda Caporael wrote memorably: 'The utmost caution is necessary in assessing the physical and mental states of people dead for hundreds of years.'

Their lives remain sketchily preserved only in public records. Where one is dealing with lives possibly touched by ergotism, a toxic state that affects victims mentally as well as physically, then an understanding of Salem's social atmosphere in early spring of 1692 is fundamental to understanding the directions the crisis took. A belief in witchcraft was a wholly accepted tenet of the Puritans' religious doctrine. The malignant workings of Satan and his wicked apostate angels were as real to the early New England colonists as their belief in God. Yet the low incidence of trials for witchcraft in the region before 1692 indicates that the Puritans did not, as a matter of course, resort to accusations of witchery in order to deal with implacable differences or baffling events.

The behaviour of the afflicted girls was apparently well known in the early spring. It was because of the consternation felt by some villagers that Mary Sibley organized the making of the rye witch-cake described earlier. This confection was fed to a dog, in the belief that the animal's reaction would indicate the presence in the community of anything spiritually unclean. Although it is not known how the dog reacted, Caporael finds it plausible that the creature did have convulsions. The witch-cake experiment, therefore, rather than any magic tricks by Tituba, may well have triggered subsequent events.

Investigators have generally overlooked the importance of the witch cake. The Reverend Parris's denouncement of Mary Sibley's action is in his church records. He writes that until the making of the cake, there was no suspicion of witchcraft, no reports of apparitions. Once a community member had gone 'to the Devil for help against the Devil', to use Parris's words, the emotional climate for witch trials had been created. The afflicted girls, who had made no previous mention of witchcraft, seized on a root cause for their behaviour, and so did the rest of the community. The girls accused three persons as being witches, thereby making their affliction a matter for the legal system rather than the medical establishment or their own families.

The records of the trials in the meeting house describe many interruptions, almost always by the afflicted girls. Usually they were outbursts where they described spectres invisible to the court and what those creatures were doing; or they gave jibbering, disjointed accounts of familiars – agents of the devil in animal form – and their odious tricks. Often the girls suffered violent fits that they and others attributed to torture by apparitions. The 'spectral evidence' put forward at the trials appears to have been a cocktail of illusory experiences and perceptual disturbances of the kind induced by ergotism. The convulsions, as described in the public record, were epileptiform – a sudden abnormal discharge of cerebral neurons, causing convulsions of arms and legs, howling, clamping of the jaw and incontinence, followed by amnesia after the event.

Physical symptoms of the eight afflicted girls and many of the older accusers are consistent with a diagnosis of convulsive ergot poisoning. Sensations of pinching, throttling, pricking with pins and biting by the apparitions of the accused constituted the girls' standard testimony in almost every examination and trial. Throttling can indicate the involvement of ergot with involuntary muscular fibres, which is typical of ergot poisoning; the biting, pinching and pricking could be a reference to the just-under-the-skin crawling and tingling sensations reported by victims of ergotism. Common among the depositions of the accusers were complaints of vomiting and 'bowels almost pulled out'; ergotism commonly causes vomiting and a tearing pain in the lower abdomen.

Examined in the light of a physiological hypothesis, a lot more of the evidence can be interpreted as symptomatic of ergotism's occasionally powerful hallucinatory features. After being throttled and near strangled by the apparition of a witch who sat on his chest, John Londer told the court that a black thing came through the window and stood close to his face. 'The body of it looked like a monkey, only the feet were like cocks' feet, with claws, and the face somewhat more like a man's than a monkey ... the thing spoke to me ...'

Joseph Bayley lived outside Salem at Newbury. According to C. W. Upham in *Salem Witchcraft*, en route to Boston the Bayleys probably spent the night at the home of Thomas Putnam. In the morning, as the Bayleys left Salem and were passing the Proctor house, Joseph said he sustained a 'very hard blow' on his chest, even though no one was near him at the time. He could see the Proctors, John and Elizabeth, who were actually in prison in Boston at the time on charges of witchcraft; Bayley's wife said she saw only 'a little maid'. Bayley suffered another blow on the chest, powerful enough this time to make him dismount from his horse; as he did so he saw a woman striding towards him. Again his wife told him she saw nothing unusual. As he got back on his horse he saw a cow where a moment before he had seen the woman. Nothing else unusual happened in the course of the trip, but when the Bayleys got home, Joseph was 'pinched and nipped by something invisible for some time'. There is no record of what Bayley ate at the Putnams' house, or how much, and it cannot be said with certainty that he even stayed there – Upham says that the Bayleys *probably* spent the night at the home of Thomas Putnam. Nevertheless, Caporael believes the content of the statement suggests ergot. Bayley had a feeling of crawling on his skin and disturbed sensations, plus the muscular contractions typical of ergot poisoning.

When the witchcraft episode came to an end in the late autumn of 1692, twenty people had been killed by order of law, and at least two others had died in prison. It cannot be too heavily emphasized, in the context of Linnda Caporael's hypothesis, that every conviction in the Salem trials was obtained on the basis of the controversial 'spectral evidence' – the seeing of visions. It is also significant, given the weather's effect on ergot development, that a commonly expressed view of the 1692 outbreak of witchcraft is that it ended unexpectedly, without apparent reason (but it ended in a drought). Increase Mather, father of Cotton Mather, preached a sermon on 3 October 1692 urging that the courts demand evidence much more conclusive than apparitions or the test of touch; this was simply a stronger restatement of the clergy's advice to the court on 15 June. Throughout the examinations, justifications for dismissing spectral evidence had been raised regularly by the accused and several of the people defending them. Normal people, no matter how inured they were to the notion that supernatural evil could exist in their midst, were bound to be unhappy about spiteful and easily concocted evidence being accepted without proof.

From the start there had been a strong undertow of opposition to the trials themselves. Linnda Caporael discovered that throughout the colonies there had been virtually no support at all. Some clergy gave their approval cautiously at best; most did not approve. The Salem witchcraft affair was an incident isolated by time, place and arguably by mass toxic delusion.

It is impossible to know how widely ergotized grain may have been distributed. Salem town's food supply came from Salem village; the convictions and orders for executions were obtained in the town. Caporael speculates that the thought processes of the magistrates, all of them rational and well-respected men in Massachusetts, might have been altered. Nevins reveals in *Witchcraft in Salem Village* that in the years that followed the trials nearly all the magistrates professed openly to making judgemental mistakes.

Linnda Caporael says the post-trial documents are as suggestive of ergotism at the time of the trials as the trial documentation itself. Samuel Sewall, in a public statement made in 1696, acknowledged personal guilt because of the unsafe principles pursued by the court. The jurymen felt they had been wrong, too. A public apology delivered on behalf of all twelve made no bones about the scale of their error: 'We confess that we ourselves were not capable to understand nor able to withstand the mysterious delusion of the Powers of Darkness and Prince of the Air ... [we] do hereby declare that we justly fear that we were sadly deluded and mistaken ...'

John Hale, the minister who had been involved in the trials from the very beginning, wrote: '... such was the darkness of the day that we walked in the clouds and could not see our way.'

Ann Putnam Jr, the afflicted girl who gave accusing testimony in twenty-one cases, finally confessed publicly in 1706:

> I justly fear I have been instrumental with others though
> ignorantly and unwittingly, to bring upon myself and this
> land the guilt of innocent blood; though what was said or
> done by me against any person I can truly and uprightly
> say before God and man, I did it not for any anger, malice

or ill will to any person, for I had no such things against one of them, but what I did was ignorantly, being deluded of Satan.

If ergot was implicated in the events at Salem in 1692, it is reasonable to ask if it might have been involved in other incidents of presumed witchcraft. A superficial examination of cases concerning Old World witchcraft suggests that it was. Periodically throughout the Middle Ages and right up to the seventeenth century, the district of Lorraine in northwest France recorded outbreaks of witchcraft *and* ergotism. In the eighteenth century, clergy at Saxony debated whether convulsive ergotism indicated disease or possession by the devil. In his book *Witchcraft in Old and New England*, G. L. Kittredge describes 'a typical case' from the early seventeenth century. The evil sorcery of Alice Trevisard, alleged to be a witch, worked against her: a witness said that Alice's hands, fingers and toes 'rotted and consumed away' – a clear enough description of gangrenous ergotism. In 1762 the Royal Society diagnosed ergotism in a family in a small English village who had suffered gangrene. The head of the family did not accept that interpretation of their terrible symptoms. It had to be witchcraft, he insisted; no other explanation would do. Illness, as anyone knew, came on by debilitating stages. The onset of *this* catastrophe had been sudden, 'like a foul curse'.

Linnda Caporael acknowledges that the existence of ergot poisoning in Salem can never be conclusively proved, but her circumstantial case is persuasive. The growing conditions and the local patterns of agriculture both align with the 1692 crisis. Physical symptoms and signs of the condition are apparent from the records of the trials and other documents of the period. Distortions of perception may have been caused by ergotism, but other factors, socially and psychologically based, give the symptoms shape and meaning. Modern pharmacology shows us that the content of a hallucination (or any other perceptual disturbance) is strongly governed by the condition of mind, mood and the expectations of the sufferer. Before the episode with the witch cake, the nature of the girls' hallucinations was not known. However, after the perplexity gave way to a line of action and the ritual with the cake had been performed, a system of delusion, founded on witchcraft, was created to explain the things the girls were seeing and saying.

In her published work on the circumstantial case for ergotism at Salem, Linnda Caporael cites S. Valins and R. Nisbett, co-authors of *Attribution: Perceiving the Causes of Behaviour*, and quotes them on the factors determining sufferers' deluded explanations of what they may have seen, felt or heard:

> The intelligence of the particular patient determines the structural coherence and internal consistency of the explanation. The cultural experiences of the patient determine the content – political, religious, or scientific – of the explanation.

Knowing nothing about ergotism, and perplexed to watch their own kin run around wildly, convulse, scream with pain, see apparitions and babble senselessly, the Puritans of New England snatched an explanation from the deep pool of their traditional terrors: witchcraft.

During the mid-1980s Mary Matossian, a historian from the University of Maryland, read Linnda Caporael's paper on ergotism at Salem. Something in the text struck a chord, and as she re-read the paper she felt that Caporael's findings had much wider implications than perhaps the author had realized. With a powerful university-based scientific and statistical methodology at her disposal, Matossian set about making a systematic study of witch trials in Europe. Using climatic evidence from dendrochronology records of the geographical spread of rye-growing areas and accounts of witchcraft trials from parish records, Matossian trawled the accumulated information looking for correlations.

The results were outstanding. For the first time the history of randomly distributed witchcraft outbreaks and civilian panics started to make sense. In rye-dependent English areas such as Essex and Norfolk, when the climate was cold and wet, the incidence of witch persecution was significantly higher than at other times.

This was true all the way across Europe. By far the majority of witch trials had taken place in and around the major rye-producing region, the Rhine valley. In cold, wet years the incidence of trials climbed, and again the rise was significantly higher than at other times. Working with the appropriate records from Swabia, in south-western Germany (including a yearly record of rye prices, which suggested pressure on poor people to eat inferior grain), Matossian was able to predict close to two-thirds of the alleged witchcraft outbreaks.

Matossian felt there was a great deal more – and of more importance – to be learned from this line of research. There was evidence, much of it deduced from anecdotal sources, that Europe had known colossal outbreaks of ergotism in medieval times. In afflicted communities who depended on rye as their only source of food, the death rate could be as high as sixty or even seventy per cent of those affected. Peasant families with no available means of alleviating their suffering died slow, agonizing deaths.

In the worst years witch persecutions increased as frightened, superstitious people fought back at the evil they feared had been sent to envelop them in its pain and darkness. How many helpless, ignorant people perished with nothing that even approached an understanding of what was happening to them? Matossian's patient research began to reveal a wholesale killer going about its slaughter invisibly and unsuspected. The true mortality figures would probably never be known, but the strong possibility remains that ergot may have had an effect on history more devastating than we could ever imagine.

Matossian found herself being driven on in this area of study by the awareness, never far away, of a puzzle that had dogged her entire professional career. From 1348 to 1350 Europe had been in the grip of the plague. It was, in Matossian's words, a demographic disaster. Something between a third and a half of Europe's population died. It was not until the early seventeenth century that figures reached pre-plague levels, after which the population boomed until the mid-nineteenth century. People were dying off in numbers that actually kept the population static. What was the reason for this slow increase over 250 years? Widespread famine would not have been likely. With such a huge number of the population gone, there was plenty of land for farming. Besides, demographic experts have demonstrated that famine has never accounted overall for a static population. It was not infection, either; the deaths occurred at the times of year when common infections were dormant. It is also a fact that a thin spread of population ensures a greatly reduced risk from infectious diseases than one of normal or above-normal density. There had to be something else. Matossian suspects that it was large-scale ergot poisoning. But suspicions are shadowy entities with no foothold in science. She needed proof.

First she studied the evidence of weather for the period, using core samples and dendrochronological records. She discovered that the weather in the late Middle Ages was very cold and wet, and those were conditions that would favour the development of ergot on rye. Now she needed to refine her research criteria: she had to muster more precise data for trends not only in climate but in the population's diet, mortality and fertility. Matossian took the accumulated figures and subjected them to analysis.

Again her results were impressive, and so was the way in which she demonstrated them. She identified years when the weather would have been ideal for ergot to infest the rye, that is a very cold winter and a warm, wet summer. For those years she made a map that displayed areas of varying agricultural production, including the production of rye. On this she overlaid a map showing her data for mortality and fertility. The areas showing rye production corresponded precisely with those of high mortality.

While in Moscow conducting research from the weather archives in the Tsarist records, Matossian learned that in Russia, too, convulsive ergotism had strong traditional associations with evil; the popular name for the disease was *zilaia korcha*, the 'evil writhing'. As in Salem, there was a greater number of young victims, meaning that those making accusations of witchcraft were nearly always pre-pubescent or teenaged.

Looking further, Matossian found that Russian climate conditions and years climatically ideal for ergot growth correlated with eighty to ninety per cent mortality among those affected, an astonishing figure. Had she stumbled across the real explanation for the failure of Europe's population to grow after the disaster of 1348 to 1350? The figures began to climb again only in 1750. This was a time, Matossian points out, when rye was gradually replaced by wheat and potatoes as the staples of European diet.

The frightful significance of these assumptions may be one reason why a mass-poisoning hypothesis has never been directly addressed before. We could be approaching a fresh understanding of European history. Is it likely that ignorance and superstition blinded our ancestors to a natural scourge in their own fields of grain? If Caporael and Matossian are right, then an insignificant-looking fungus played a huge, unremarked role in altering the history of the human race in Europe.

Mary Matossian notices disturbing signs of ergot becoming a large-scale threat again. Since 1997, there has been an epidemic of ergot in sorghum agriculture – sorghum is also known as Indian millet, Guinea corn and durra. This strain of ergot originated in Africa and has spread as far as North and South America and Australia. In terms of toxic virulence, sorghum ergot is not as potent as the strain that infests rye; it does not kill human beings yet, although it is disastrous for sorghum crops. The speed of its spread, in spite of large-scale attempts to block it, demonstrates that we can do little, if anything, to contain serious infestations, whatever form they take. In the American South, where sorghum ergot has been at its most devastating, an efficient crop-drying system is to some extent keeping the fungus in check, if not eliminating it.

In one part of the world there now exists a real danger of ergot passing again to human beings. Since the collapse of the Soviet Union in 1991, and more particularly the recent collapse of the rouble, Russian agriculture has been in terrible crisis, and recent harvests have been completely inadequate. Rye remains a crucially important crop, but financial resources are not available for setting up plants for drying the harvested crops before they are stored. This level of inadequacy to control a scourge is what turned ergot into a lethal curse in medieval times.

Nothing in nature remains static for long. If we do not resist what harms us, it grows and becomes more of a threat. Professor Bertram Pockney, formerly of Suffolk University, who has been a lifelong observer of Soviet life, confirms that there is a mounting danger in the East. Dr Marco Guilami of the World Health Organization has reports of recent outbreaks of ergot poisoning in the Russian Federation and in 1997, 110 people were affected by an outbreak of ergotism in Krygestan. Danger in the East, from whatever source, has never boded well for the West.

5

THE SYPHILIS
ENIGMA

SINCE SHORTLY AFTER THE discovery of America, it has been widely accepted that the scourge of syphilis in Europe came about as part of the 'Columbian exchange', one of the gifts – along with tobacco and the potato – that the New World conferred on the Old. The long-standing explanation is that members of Columbus's expedition to the Americas caught the disease from native women; then unwittingly brought it back to Spain in 1493, triggering an epidemic that spread across Europe.

In the past few years, however, archaeologists and experts in osteophathology (the study of diseases in bone) have begun to question the orthodox stance on the history of syphilis. In support of their serious doubts they point to evidence found in ancient bones unearthed from sites all over Europe, including several in England.

Now, from the superficially unpromising location of a multi-storey car park in Kingston upon Hull, there comes evidence that has set the archaeological world buzzing. A dig has uncovered a medieval friary, and among the human remains that have lain there for hundreds of years, there may be proof that syphilis existed in Europe long before Columbus ever set sail for the New World.

First, though, a backward glance.

When AIDS was first diagnosed in 1981 and news of its catastrophic potential began to spread, moral prohibitionists could have enjoyed no more powerful boost to their main purpose in life – which is, of course, to frighten the rest of us for our own good. Very much the same must have happened in the sixteenth century when the existence and consequences of syphilis became known to the people of Europe. Here was a risk of sexual activity which could bring disgrace, deformity, madness and death to the wary and unwary alike. The ancient legend of the Giftmädchen, the poison damsel, whose love carried a deadly curse, had become a grim fact. Syphilis was the bacterial ally of Mrs Grundy.

It was also the despair of medicine. Until well into the twentieth century and the development of penicillin, there was no cure and no particularly humane treatment for syphilis. Even in 1940, a typical instruction given to British doctors ran as follows: 'In new cases of syphilis, hindrance to the initiation of treatment must be avoided. Administration of preparations of arsenic by the intravenous route should be commenced without delay.'

The health and well-being of patients was secondary to public health anxieties, most of them centred on preventing the spread of infection. Patients were, after all, degenerate types who had walked into the blades of divine retribution, or so the generally censorious thinking went, therefore they were not afforded the courtesies to which decent people were entitled. Over the centuries the arguments and theories surrounding venereal diseases have largely centred on syphilis. The names that have been pinned on the infection suggest a powerful (and usually hypocritical) undertow of disapproval in people's view of the disease, and more than a hint of racism. Mal de Napoli, Scottish sivvens, Swedish saltfluss, Morbus gallicus, French pox and Spanish pox are a tiny sampling. Although there aren't as many American nicknames for the condition, there is an anecdote about Al Capone, who was diagnosed as suffering from syphilis while he was in prison (where he subsequently died of the disease). An old prison doctor, giving Capone a thorough medical examination, pointed to one of the gangster's more prominent lesions and muttered to a colleague: 'That's a Chicago chancre.'

In the 1930s and 1940s, the physical vigour of patients was depleted and in many cases wrecked by the clinical regimes used to treat their syphilis. In many ways the attempts at cure, or containment, were as damaging as the disease itself. It was not the fastest-acting therapy in the world, either, and as time went by things would always get worse for the patient. That did not apply solely to the progress of the disease, but to the stepping-up and prolonging of the unpleasant treatment. This extract from a 1940s manual makes the point:

> Soon after treatment with arsenic compounds has commenced, the manifestations of the disease disappear rapidly. This swift improvement is found to be temporary, however, and further treatment must be applied. It is found most advantageous to supplement the course of arsenic injections with appropriate doses of mercury and potassium iodide, which should be continued over a period of two years.

Society kept its poor and ill-educated in darkness; the extent to which fear and ignorance could actually disturb the balance of the mind was recounted in 1939 by an American surgeon. This man, a practitioner of the now-outdated technique called psychosurgery – the cutting of nerve paths in the brain to 'cure' psychosis and depression – clearly did not realize just how horrible a story he was telling:

> Obsessive ideas sometimes develop from apparently rather trivial circumstances. One of our patients noticed a rash over the upper part of the chest where her telephone instrument rested. She developed the idea that she had an incurable disease, syphilis, and from then on for twelve years was completely miserable, constantly obsessed with the idea. Inquiry into the circumstances surrounding the rash, which lasted for only three days, showed that at just this time she had been kissed passionately by her sister's boyfriend. The mixture of pleasure and guilt that attended this experience was possibly the genesis of the obsessive rumination, reinforced by the unexplained appearance of the rash, and she got over it only after her second prefrontal lobotomy. Previous attempts to deal with the chain of events leading up to the neurosis were absolutely defeated by the insistence upon the presence of the incurable disease.

The persistent notion that a person's authority in a particular field gives him or her the automatic right to domineer and intimidate is illustrated in another news story from the United States. In the early years of the Second World War, Dr I. K. Wallis, a syphilologist (a specialist in the study of syphilis), devised a method for deterring young people from experimenting with sex. Travelling from town to town and enjoying the unstinting support of local youth organizations, he set about purging the youth of America of their unhealthy tendencies before depravity had a chance to take hold. His technique stands comparison with the aversion therapy inflicted on Alex in Anthony Burgess's *A Clockwork Orange*. Dr Wallis would seat twenty or thirty teenage boys or girls (always one sex or the other, never mixed) in front of a large projection screen. In a short preliminary talk he would explain that what he was about to show them was absolutely real, and that it fearlessly illustrated what happened to people who behaved improperly with members of the opposite sex before they were married. If his audience consisted of girls, he would show them a ten-minute 16-millimetre movie, in colour, of women with advanced stages of syphilis and gonorrhoea. The film showed these unfortunate souls as they underwent painful, sloughing procedures in American venereal disease clinics, in prison medical units and field hospitals run by the military. If the audience were boys, they would be shown a film of venereally diseased men having similarly vicious procedures applied to their diseased parts. The horrible images were accompanied by a soundtrack of people moaning, groaning and screaming. No explanation of the procedures was provided; there was simply the evidence of the images and the terrible soundtrack. Dr Wallis is on record as saying that his campaign against promiscuity was a resounding success, even though liberal public opinion caused him to abandon it after a two-year run: 'As they filed out past me I could always tell from my young audiences' faces that they had been sickened and deeply shocked.'

This kind of deranged bullying echoes the professional ignorance that often lay behind atrocities committed on patients with venereal infections, especially in the centuries before antibiotics. Syphilis and other infections resulting from 'excessive pursuit of the veneries' were variously treated with leeches, abrasive pastes, phlebotomy (bloodletting), burning and blistering with irritants. Other regimes could involve purging with a variety of herbal laxatives, or cleansing of the bowels with acidic clysters – enemas – often administered by means of a pig's bladder and a length of greased pipe.

Many sufferers during the early centuries after its appearance in Europe, kept their syphilitic infection a secret and chose either to treat themselves or simply to suffer and trust to providence. Better to do either one of those, many believed, than to undergo the misery and expense of treatment by barber surgeons and backstreet healers. Old records and the evidence of archaeology show that although some infected people survived untreated through the early epidemics of syphilis, and a few even experienced spontaneous cures, many others suffered years of unspeakable misery before they succumbed to the ravaging final stages of the disease.

The eighteenth and nineteenth centuries were little better. In spite of the new-style doctors with their high-sounding disciplines, syphilis continued to maim, kill and generate untold misery. Moralists still condemned sufferers as dancers with the devil, while healers, scarcely hindered by ethical issues, devised new hardships in the hope of hitting on a system of treatment that actually helped the patient.

Often the avoidance of disease was made difficult by plain lasciviousness. In women this could degenerate into a medical complaint, known to specialist physicians of the eighteenth century as a raging womb. Needless to say, there were remedies; the following is from the *General Practice of Physic*, published in 1763:

> Salacity in women, attended with impudence, restlessness and a delirium, is called the *furor uterinus*. I should choose to refer this disorder to the head, as there is sometimes a melancholy, and sometimes a maniacal delirium. The patients delight to talk obscenely, and solicit men to satisfy their desires, both by words and gestures.

It arises from a too great sensibility, or inflammation of the pudenda, or parts wherein the venereal stimulus resides, which are chiefly the clitoris and vagina; or the too great abundance and acrimony of the fluids of those parts; or both these causes may exist together.

In the *delirium maniacum*, the patient is intirely shameless; in the *melancholicum* more reserved, and her folly is confined to fewer objects.

It may proceed from the abuse of hot aperitives; thus sal ammoniac, borax and cantharides have produced it; from powerful liquors in hot and bilious constitutions; sometimes from difficult and suppressed menses; from remedies given against sterility. Musk dissolved in aromatic oil, and rubbed on the *membrum virile*, has raised a phlogosis [inflammation] in the vagina, whence a *furor uterinus* ensued.

It is difficult of cure in those whose menses are difficult at first; in inveterate cases; in old subjects. It is easier cured, when the *furor uterinu*s is essential, and the delirium symptomatic, than when the delirium is essential, and the *furor* symptomatic. The maniacal delirium is harder to manage than the melancholic. If it continues a month or two, the fault of the brain becomes obstinate, for it degenerates into real madness.

The indications of cure are to diminish the heat and sensibility of the affected parts. To cool, sweeten and dilute the blood, and to render it balsamic; or to pursue both intentions at once.

The first indication is answered by frequent and copious bleedings, as in an incipient madness; even to eight times in two days, if nothing forbids; if she faints, there is no danger. She must likewise be purged, as mad folks are, with salap, scammony, diagrid. The dose must be increased one third, as being hard to purge. Emetics are also good, for they evacuate the bile, which abates the acrimony of the humours.

In a *delirium melancholicum* lawful coition may be admitted, for I knew a woman of some consequence run to the guard-room, and return perfectly cured.

Bloodletting, which has appealed to mankind as a medicinal *sine qua non* since the days of cave-dwelling, had its own nineteenth-century specialists. An influential physicians' textbook of the time was the *Cyclopaedia of Practical Medicine*, which recommended bloodletting in cases of syphilis and any other 'recalcitrant afflictions showing a tendency to thicken the humor of the blood'. Often a doctor would resort to what was known as local bloodletting in order to relieve the agony of skull and long-bone lesions in syphilis; the *Cyclopaedia* offered comment and instruction on the technique, with a couple of alternatives typical of the period:

Local bloodletting is chiefly applicable as an auxiliary to general bloodletting, and in local diseases in which general bloodletting is not required. In cases of inflammation within the head, chest or abdomen, after the due abstraction of blood generally, the local abstraction of blood is very often employed most opportunely. The second remedy secures the benefit, which the first had conferred. In regard to the application of a large number of leeches in such cases, a few words of caution are, however, necessary. The loss of the blood so withdrawn is not always well borne when the lance has been used efficiently just before; and if applied late at night, the flow of blood is apt to continue unheeded, until an undue quantity of blood has been poured out. Both these events have occurred, and led to unavailing regret.

Cupping is, generally speaking, a more efficient remedy than leeching. It is most appropriately applied to the nape of the neck, behind the ears, to the temples, to the various parts of the chest, over the region of the liver, the kidney, etc. To the softer parts of the abdomen, leeches must be applied.

Both these remedies are peculiarly efficacious in cases in which the powers of the whole system have been duly subdued by general bloodletting, without the removal of the symptoms of the local disease. Only the quantity so withdrawn after the general bloodletting must not be too great.

A prevailing school of medical thought in the eighteenth and nineteenth centuries held that the elimination of syphilis in a patient could only be achieved by means as atrocious as the disease itself. Signs of remission in the infection had to be taken as the go-ahead for a vigorous campaign against the retreating enemy, just to be sure it didn't come back. This extract is from a medical paper of 1833:

When on the tentative road to recovery, the sufferer from syphilis will often derive benefit from the use of the nitromuriatic acid bath. This is prepared by adding two ounces of strong hydrochloric and one ounce of strong nitric acid to two gallons of water, at a temperature of 96 or 98 degrees. Both feet are to be placed in the bath, while the legs and thighs, the region over the liver, and both arms, are sponged alternately, or the abdomen may be swathed in flannel soaked in the water. The process is to be continued for half an hour night and morning. It is absolutely necessary that a wooden tub should be used, as the acid very soon destroys any ordinary metal bath. The sponges and towels should be placed in cold water after use, or they too will soon be destroyed.

If excoriating, cutting, burning or otherwise injuring the surface of the sufferer's body failed to produce a cure, the healers could turn to a daunting range of internal medicines. The following remedy of 1790 for women suffering a high fever in syphilis, apart from being useless, calls for some clarification: an emmenagogue is any drug or compound that increases menstrual flow; a hectic is a fever; an aloetic is any medicine containing aloes as its main ingredient.

This circumstance requires immediate bleeding in the foot and resolvent decoctions of chicory-roots, leaves of sow-thistle, daisy- and elder-flowers, forbearing all strong emmenagogues. But if the patient has laboured long under a hectic, and is greatly weakened and emaciated, bleeding must be omitted.

If the menses are stopped, and there is a hectic with an atrophy, cough, diarrhoea, universal languor of the whole body, and a slow consuming heat, no emmenagogues must be used, but directly the contrary. The same may be said of the stoppage of the periodical flux of the bleeding chanker, for the giving of aloetics in this case has hurried many out of the world.

The 1833 edition of the *Cyclopaedia of Practical Medicine* offered instruction in a new and particularly unpleasant therapy that had a vast range of uses, among them the reduction of inflammation in the genital sores caused by syphilis. One can only guess at the amount of distress and harm the innovation caused.

The simplest method of applying electricity to the cure of disease is to present the member to the prime conductor of the machine, and thus cause it to receive a succession of sparks; or, what is more convenient, to place the patient on a chair, and convey to him the sparks by means of a director connected with the conductor by a chain. The patient may manage the director while the operator works the machine.

A second mode consists in placing the patient upon an insulating stool, putting him in connexion, through means of a chain or metallic rod, with the prime conductor, and drawing sparks from the seat of disease or pain by simply presenting to such part the knuckle, or, should the operator dislike receiving the spark himself, an uninsulated director. This method is that usually adopted by those experienced in the medicinal administration of electricity. The force of the spark is proportionate to its length, so that, by properly diminishing this, its strength may be reduced to any required standard.

No reference to the medical literature of the nineteenth century would be complete without at least a glance at *Sexual Physiology* by R. T. Trall, published in 1866. Like many others in his field, this American doctor used his textbook as a platform for his prejudices, many of them alarmingly repressive. Like the syphilologist Dr Wallis, Trall had very firm views on where carnality had its roots, and he wasn't afraid to lay the blame squarely where it belonged:

> The manner in which the great majority of American children are fed, if it does not ruin their digestive organs and render them dyspeptics or consumptives, is sure to produce permanent congestion, with constant irritation in the pelvic viscera, resulting in a precocious development and morbid intensity of sexual stimulation. Tea, coffee, flesh meats, to say nothing of the abominations of the baker and confectioner, are sufficient to account for the early tendency to sexual dissipation and debauchery manifested by a large portion of the children in our primary schools. Many a parent, now confident in the purity and safety of his own son or daughter, might be appalled if he should investigate this subject.

The question of where syphilis came from has been called the most controversial issue in medical history, but before examining that topic it is useful first to look at the disease itself. A recent American survey concluded that people in general have only a vague notion of what the infection is and how it is manifested in its victims. Only a minority of those interviewed could describe any of the symptoms, and it would seem that the strong element of taboo surrounding the disease, evident from the literature of past centuries, has lasted to the present day.

There was a time when people could scarcely utter the word 'syphilis', which, as the journalist Benjamin Skelton pointed out in 1930, 'has always carried shivery overtones of licentiousness and filth'. The name of the disease originated in the title of a Latin poem, '*Syphilis, sive Morbus Gallicus*', published in 1530 by Girolamo Fracastoro of Verona, a doctor, astronomer and poet. The word 'syphilis' is used in the poem as the name of the disease, as well as being the name of the main character, a shepherd said to be the first syphilitic.

The disease is caused by an organism called *Treponema pallidum*. It is a corkscrew-shaped microbe capable of spontaneous movement. It usually enters the body by close sexual contact, getting in through tiny nicks and tears in the body's mucus-coated inner surfaces. It can also be transmitted to an unborn baby through the bloodstream of an infected mother during the later stages of pregnancy.

Syphilis has three stages, each of which has very distinct clinical features. The primary stage in both men and women is established when a small hard pimple, referred to as a papule, develops between two to four weeks after the infection has entered the body; usually the papule appears on the penis in males and on the labia or cervix in females. Days later it breaks down and becomes a painless, hard-edged ulcer known as a venereal chancre. Throughout this time no pain or discomfort is associated with the infection, and the primary chancre usually heals in a few weeks.

The secondary stage comes two or three months after the healing of the chancre. There are combined symptoms, such as a sore throat, fever, severe pains in the joints and a general sensation of debility. More specific signs often include a skin rash that covers the whole body, including the palms of the hands and the soles of the feet, but not the face; condylomas, which are also called syphilitic warts and appear at various moist sites on the body; clusters of ulcers in the mouth and on the external genital organs.

The signs of secondary syphilis diminish after a few months, but in as many as a fifth of all sufferers they come back during a period known as early latency. After a year the period called late latency begins, and this may continue for many years before the late stages of syphilis start to show.

In the tertiary stage there is a distressing involvement of the skin and bones. Non-malignant tumours called gummas – because of the gummy nature of their contents – can develop anywhere on the skin, and quite often at sites of injury. Internally, they are found in the skull, the tibia, the fibula and the clavicle (collarbone), although any bone can be affected. Other gummas arise in the liver and the testicles. At this time neurosyphilis – syphilis of the central nervous system – can occur, usually bringing with it a clutch of complex secondary diseases. It is not uncommon for the brain itself to be affected, leading to the condition called paresis, also known as Bayle's disease; it is also referred to by some medical professionals as 'general paralysis of the insane'. Paresis is marked by progressive dementia, continual trembling, disturbed speech and increasing weakness in the muscles. In a large number of cases, paresis has a preliminary stage where the patient is highly irritable, but in time this gives way to elation, delusions of grandeur and a fairly rapid detachment from reality.

When a child is born with syphilis, the infection becomes evident between the second and sixth week after birth. The early signs are a particularly unpleasant nasal discharge, lesions on the skin and the mucous membranes, and a general failure to thrive like a normal child. Signs of late syphilis do not appear until after two years; they take the form of so-called 'stigmata', which are signs of early damage to developing teeth, long bones and other bodily structures. Further signs of late syphilis in the child are the same as those in adult tertiary syphilis. Today syphilis is treated with penicillin, which kills the spirochaetes.

There are in fact four infections caused by the bacterial genus *Treponema*: they are venereal syphilis, which has just been described, endemic syphilis, yaws and pinta. Much of the confused history of syphilis arose from early misdiagnosis or confusion of one disease with another.

Endemic syphilis is a form of syphilis which, as its name suggests, is found regularly among certain human groupings and is not transmitted sexually. Invariably, it is spread in circumstances of poor hygiene; the organism enters the system through skin abrasions. The disease, which particularly affects Arab children, rarely produces a primary lesion, as venereal syphilis does, although the late stages of the two diseases are indistinguishable. Treatment of the endemic form is the same as for venereal syphilis.

Yaws is the second most widespread treponemal disease (syphilis being the first), and it is spread by direct contact, again usually among children. As with endemic syphilis, the organism enters the system through damaged areas of the skin. The incubation period can be weeks or months, after which primary inflammation develops at the point where the infection entered the body. Soon afterwards, multiple raised, hard lesions appear on the skin, usually involving the palms of the hands and the soles of the feet. There may also be bone involvement, with the infection invading the long bones and the bones of the hand. In the late stage of yaws, the infection in the bones can accelerate, causing severe disfigurement and destruction, especially in the skull and facial bones, the finger joints and the long bones. There can be a latent period between the early and late phases of this disease, just as there is with venereal syphilis. Treatment with penicillin, together with improved hygiene, has considerably reduced the numbers and severity of cases of yaws.

Pinta, which is restricted to Central and South America, closely resembles endemic syphilis. The organism enters through damaged skin, and the primary lesion is an itchy red pimple, usually on the hand or the foot. In the later stages, more of the lesions can appear. Later still, symmetrical slate-blue patches appear on the face, hands and feet. Eventually, the patches lose all pigment. Early treatment with penicillin is the only remedy.

Given that nowadays we have no doubt about how inhumane one race or class of people can be to another, it is worthwhile at this point to record an instance of spectacular medical infamy, known as the Tuskegee Syphilis Study, conducted over a forty-year period in the name of scientific enquiry.

The project, which ran from 1932 to 1972 and was carried out by the United States Public Health Service (PHS), followed the progress of untreated syphilis in black American males. The purpose of the research was to determine if syphilis was responsible for cardiovascular damage more often than damage to the central nervous system, and to find out if the natural course of the disease in black men was appreciably different from that in white men. To muster recruits for the study, the PHS engaged the help of the eminent Tuskegee Institute at Macon county, Alabama. Eventually, 412 patients infected with syphilis and 204 uninfected control patients were signed up, all of them impoverished, uneducated sharecroppers from Macon county. The original study was planned to last no longer than nine months.

No one working on the project told the recruits that they had syphilis, or that the disease could be passed on through sexual intercourse. They were told they suffered from 'bad blood', an imprecise local term which referred to a whole range of ailments. At first, treatment was part of the study; several recruits were given arsenic, mercury and bismuth. However, when the project produced no useful data, those running the study decided to follow the course of the syphilis in the patients until their deaths.

All treatment was withdrawn. Even in the 1940s, when a cure came along in the form of penicillin, it was withheld from the men, and twenty-five years later it was still being withheld from them. This was a violation of government legislation that made the treatment of venereal disease compulsory. Over a hundred of the recruits died of tertiary syphilis.

The Tuskegee Syphilis Study ended in 1972 when the project's unprincipled methods were exposed in a feature in the *Washington Star*. A class-action suit (a lawsuit undertaken by one or more plaintiffs on behalf of themselves, anyone else having an identical interest in the alleged wrong) was brought against the federal government; an out-of-court settlement of ten million dollars was made in 1974. In the same year the United States Congress introduced the National Research Act, which requires institutional review boards to approve any studies that involve human subjects.

For many years now there has been heated controversy over the origin and antiquity of syphilis. For roughly five hundred years it was widely accepted that the discovery of America and the spread of syphilis in Europe occurred more or less at the same time. Positive references to the disease in European literature appeared only after the return of Columbus and his crew from the New World.

The written history of the disease begins in 1495, at the siege of Naples. An incredibly contagious and painful new plague broke out among the troops and camp followers of Charles VIII of France, who was besieging Naples in pursuit of his claim to the kingdom. Within only three years the whole of Europe had been stricken with the malady. Terror, hysteria and horror, unparalleled until the time of AIDS, led to panic legislation in country after country as desperate attempts were made to bring the monstrosity under control. Its victims in Paris were put under curfew, and any foreigners who were located were put on twenty-four hours' notice to leave the city. All Scots suffering from the disease were shipped, under royal proclamation, to an island in the Firth of Forth, where they would either recover or die; if they recovered but looked in any way disfigured, they were branded on the forehead. Russia put a *cordon sanitaire* around its boundaries as a means of keeping the disease out.

So where did it come from? The Columbian hypothesis, supported and defended by many distinguished authorities, maintains that syphilis originated in the Americas and was passed to the sailors of the *Niña, Pinta* and *Santa Maria* by Native American women who had sexual relations with Columbus's sailors. Dr Bruce Rothschild, Director of the Arthritis Center of North-Eastern Ohio, and a powerful adherent of the Columbian hypothesis, has been looking for evidence to support his stance in the Dominican Republic in the West Indies. It is a region that occupies the eastern part of the island of Hispaniola, where Columbus and his expedition first made landfall in the New World.

'The question is,' says Rothschild, 'is syphilis a disease that started in the New World and was transferred to the old, or did Columbus's crew have something to do with the reverse phenomenon? Well, if you look at skeletons in North America, you often find evidence of syphilis prior to the days of Columbus. But that's a much further jump than having the *smoking gun* – the evidence right from here, an area where you know Columbus landed.'

The Dominican Republic has numerous archaeologic sites and among them are several that actually date from the period when Columbus arrived. 'There are some superbly dated sites from the time of five hundred to a thousand years ago,' Rothschild says. 'These sites are perfect, because if syphilis is present in them, then we know that people Columbus met here certainly had the disease.'

George Armelagos, an academic and another supporter of the Columbian standpoint, points to the sparseness of so-called cases of syphilis in Europe before the time of Columbus.

'What I would expect to find,' he says, 'is not only the fact that you have syphilis in an individual, but that you find it within the population and within a region. If these people are in social contact, they're in sexual contact, and so the disease should be widespread.'

By roughly the year 1500, syphilis had reached epidemic proportions in Europe. The rapid spread of the infection across the continent strongly suggests that the disease was attacking a population that had not been exposed to it before, and therefore had no immunity.

The pre-Columbian hypothesis, on the other hand, says that syphilis was present in Europe before Columbus ever set sail; at that time, say the supporters of this view, the disease was never distinguished from leprosy. It was not until the 1490s that syphilis was identified as a separate infection.

The earliest document proposing that syphilis had an American origin came from G. Fernandez de Oviedo, a well-respected observer and historiographer. In his *Summary*, which he addressed to the Emperor Charles V in 1525, he established firmly that the venereal disease – called *buas* by him, instead of *bubas*, which was the name the Spanish gave syphilis at that time – came from the island of Hispaniola. In a chapter describing a medicinal wood used by the natives to treat syphilis, he stated:

Your Majesty may rest assured that this disease came from the Indies. Although it is quite common among the Indians, it is not so dangerous there as it is here (in Spain). The Indians in the islands cure themselves very easily with this wood, in Tierra Firme they use other herbs or things they know, for they are great herbalists. The first time this disease was seen, it was after Admiral D. Christopher Columbus discovered the Indies, and returned to these parts. Some Christians who came with him and were present in that discovery, and those who were on the second voyage, who went in greater number, brought this plague, and from them other people were contaminated; later in the year 1495, when the Great Captain D. Gonzalo Fernandez de Cordova went to Italy with people to support young King Ferdinand of Naples against King Charles of France, he of the big head, by command of the Catholic Sovereigns D. Ferdinand and Da. Isabella of immortal memory, your Majesty's grandparents, the disease was carried with some of those Spaniards and was the first time it was seen in Italy. Since that was the time when the French under the said King Charles passed it (to Italy) the Italians called it the French disease; and the French call it the Neapolitan disease, because they had not seen it either until that war. From there it spread all over Christendom and passed into Africa by means of some men and women touched by this illness. The disease is contracted most by intercourse of man with woman, as it has been seen many times. And likewise by eating from the same plates and drinking from the same glasses and cups used by those who have the disease, and even more by sleeping on the same sheets and bedclothes which they used to sleep. This disease is so severe and painful that no man can help seeing so many people, rotten and turned into Saint Lazarus because of this malady; furthermore many people have died of it. Few Christians who associate and have intercourse with Indian women have scaped from this danger ...

The evidence that for many has clinched the issue of America's place in the story of syphilis is a Renaissance volume, of which it is believed only three copies remain. This is the *Treatise Against the Serpentine Malady*, published in 1542 by R. Diaz de Isla, a Spanish surgeon, equivalent to a present-day consultant, who worked at the All Saints Hospital at Lisbon. He maintained that he had treated over 20,000 patients with *bubas*, among them men from Columbus's crew, and had suffered the disease himself. (It is worth noting that over the centuries medical personnel working with syphilitic patients have been known to pick up the disease through minor skin injuries.) One modern authority has gone on record to say that every line in de Isla's book deserves careful thought, because he makes it possible to establish a calendar of the disease and its spread and effects worldwide. In addition to that, de Isla's observations are so meticulous and attentive to detail that they make the nature of the epidemic perfectly clear. The work provides confirmation that *bubas* came from Hispaniola with Columbus's men; that the disease was highly contagious; that among the Indians it was an everyday infection and quite benign, but among the Spaniards it was devastatingly severe. De Isla treated the first cases to arrive in Spain from America. He watched the alarming speed with which the disease spread – in his estimation a million people throughout Europe became infected. Here is de Isla in his own words, edited to clarify certain points:

> I learned by experience the remedies of the serpentine malady that came from the Hispaniola island ... its cure was soon found, using mercury, and about twenty years later the cure with the *palo* [the medicinal wood more often called *guayacan*] became known, used in ancient times by the people at the Hispaniola island. They cure more people with this disease and all sort of ailments [at the All Saints Hospital in Lisbon] than in any other hospital in Europe ... This serpentine malady appeared and was seen in Spain the year of the Lord one thousand four hundred and ninety-three in the city of Barcelona: the said city was infested, and in consequence the rest of Europe, and the universe, all parts known and communicated. The said disease had its origin and was born from the beginning of times in the island now called Hispaniola ... This malady was seen in the navy of the Admiral [Columbus] in a pilot from Palos named Pinçon, and in some others where the disease developed ... It was an ailment never seen by the Spaniards or known to them ... The Indians of the Hispaniola island in ancient times, in the same way we say here *bubas*, pains, abscesses and ulcers, they say likewise of this disease *guaynaras*, and *hipas*, and *taybas*, and *ycas* ... This disease is ... severe, one which infests and corrupts the flesh and breaks and rots the bones and shortens and twists the nerves ... It has caused so much damage that there is not a village in Europe with one hundred neighbours without ten of them dead of that ailment.

During the Enlightenment, an eighteenth-century philosophical movement that placed heavy stress on the need for people to be rational, the syphilis debate flared in Europe with new energy. An upsurge of discussion about the disease was fuelled by a book written by the Frenchman C. de Pauw entitled *Philosophical Researches about the Americans*, published in 1768. De Pauw's interest in natural history as well as philosophy had drawn him to a study of Americans after he read an account of their shortage of four-legged animals. His previous books about the Chinese, the Egyptians and the Greeks were generally acclaimed. But in this American book, as one critic put it, de Pauw had tried rather too hard to persuade world opinion that in America nature had entirely degenerated, and that included all its living elements – plants, animals and humans.

The opening pages of de Pauw's study quoted an old legend that said the American iguana was 'an animal so pernicious to those who eat it that they become infested with the venereal disease'. He rejected the learned opinion held by many that Negroes brought syphilis from Africa to America, although a few pages further on he wrote about the endemic nature of yaws, or Guinea malady as he called it, in Africa. In the first chapter, making reference to syphilis, de Pauw wrote:

> It is known with absolute certainty that it appeared after the time Christopher Columbus's crew and above all one called Margarite and a friar by the name of Buellio brought the venereal disease from Santo Domingo ... The inhabitants of the Antilles, where the venereal disease is found more often, say it came from the American Continent, and those from the Continent assert it came from the Antilles ... but everybody agrees they have been

afflicted with this ailment since time immemorial. The first European of distinction who caught the American disease was King Francis I; but before this took place in 1547 the disease had caused immense havoc on our continent; the speed of its propagation was amazing; the Moors expelled from Spain inoculated the Asiatics and the Africans. In less than two years it went from Barcelona up to Northern France. In 1496 the Parliament of Paris with all Chambers in session issued the celebrated edict forbidding any citizen with the American disease to appear in the streets under penalty of imprisonment, ordering under the same penalty that every foreigner infected should leave the city within twenty-four hours. Two years later it can be seen that the contagion was manifesting itself in Saxony; at least the students at Leipzig argued about the cause of the venereal disease which up to 1498 they did not know; they will use then insulting language among themselves, and will discuss in barbarous Latin about it, using all sort of arguments, but they will not cure a single patient.

De Pauw explained that he checked very carefully several of the early descriptions of syphilis, particularly in the work of one J. Le Maire, and then wrote:

> ... it can be noticed that the main symptoms accompanying then this epidemic disease in humans have completely disappeared in our days. We almost dare to believe that these symptoms have been mitigating from one century to

another and are going to extinguish themselves during its propagation ... The amount of remedies used by the people of those lands in order to arrest its progress, proves without any doubt that the venereal disease originated in America; they used over sixty different drugs against it, and were forced to learn them in the face of its imminent danger. It would be absolutely absurd to maintain that the Americans searched for such a variety of remedies to cure a disease unknown to them. Oviedo, who according to Fallopio became infected at Naples, was intelligent enough to understand that his disease had come from the West Indies. He then went to find the most powerful remedies; he travelled there to confirm he was right about it; the savages of Santo Domingo as soon as they saw him knew he was contaminated and showed him the Guayacan tree. It was because of his suffering that Oviedo became a happy man and made a large fortune in Spain; he took there the resins, barks and wood of Guayacan and their genuine preparation according to the American procedures. Carpi, who discovered in Italy the virtues of mercury, became one of the wealthiest men of his time, and his luxury surpassed that of famous Princes ...

De Pauw then added more observations, all of them to the effect that syphilis had its origin in America.

People who argue nowadays for the pre-Columbian hypothesis – that syphilis existed in Europe before the discovery of America – are fewer, and so are their proofs. Their principal claim that syphilis was misdiagnosed in Europe as leprosy has been countered by the suggestion that, if that were so, present-day excavations of cemeteries at European leper colonies should uncover evidence of syphilis: no such finds are recorded.

In 1932 Herbert U. Williams decided to review the existing 'proof' of pre-Columbian syphilis, or as much of it as he could lay hands on. First he made a careful study of the bones of more than five hundred skeletons of people in modern times who were known to have died of syphilis, or to have been seriously infected by the disease at some stage in their lives. Williams's purpose in studying these bones was to establish firmly the true signs of syphilitic infection, as distinct from the marks left by trauma or other diseases. Having gone through the severe discipline of that task, he then examined the available archaeological skeletons that purported to show signs of pre-Columbian syphilis. He found that many cases had been misdiagnosed; a number of reported cases of syphilis-ravaged skeletons from ancient Egypt were in fact proved to have been mutilated, after death, by rodents and insects.

In the end, Williams reckoned that only five cases of reputed pre-Columbian or 'Old World' syphilis were even halfway likely to be the real thing. Three of the cases came from France: there was a humerus and an ulna from the valley of the Marne, an ulna, a femur and a fragment of a femur from the St-Germain museum, and a tibia from Solutre. He found that the previous diagnosis of syphilis in these cases was at best questionable. Another case was represented by a tibia and fibula from Japan; these had previously been documented as being 2,500 years old, but Williams disputed that. He examined the bones with particular care and concluded that the lesions on them could as believably have been caused by trauma or healed osteomyelitis. The final case was a femur and tibia from the ancient country of Nubia, which were dated to 100 BC. Williams was able to examine only the illustrations of these bones; he concluded that the argument for syphilis was plausible, but it was just as likely that periostitis inflammation of the fibrous coating on the bones – had been the cause of the lesions. Williams's interpretation of the five cases was later assessed by a number of other experts in the field, and they all agreed with his findings.

There has been other interesting but inconclusive evidence from Europe. Examination of the skull of an adult female from Spitalfields Market in London revealed star-shaped scars of *caries sicca* (see description later), which support a diagnosis of syphilis. However, the pre-Columbian chronology appended to the skull was very possibly wrong; historical records showed that the site where the skull was found had been part of the cemetery at the church of St Mary Spittle, which had been in use from 1197 until 1537. Writing in the *Journal of Archaeological Sciences* in 1975, investigator Don Brothwell declared that it was a remarkable coincidence that the woman succumbed to syphilis within thirty-five years of the disease making its appearance in London. Brothwell's view cannot be ignored or rejected unless more convincing evidence is put forward to show that the skull really is pre-Columbian. The best-documented case from western Europe is a tibia with the spread-out markings of osteitis (inflammation of the substance of bone), and a frontal bone from a skull with the classic star-shaped scars of *caries sicca*. The material came from St Helen's-on-the-Wall at medieval York, and carbon dating confirmed that these bones were interred before Columbus sailed to the Americas.

In 1992 M. and R. Henneberg and J. Coleman Carter reported in *National Geographic Research & Exploration* that they had found evidence of treponemal infection in an early Greek colony at Metaponto in southern Italy. The bones in question were poorly preserved, however, and even those reporting the find admitted that their diagnosis must be treated as tentative; they went on to say that there was little hope of their ever being able to prove their interpretation conclusively. George Armalegos, of the Department of Anthropology at Emory University in Atlanta,

Georgia, has commented that the bone changes recorded at Metaponto look like the effects of anaemia or thalassaemia, a blood-destroying hereditary anaemia common in malarial areas of the world.

In 1971 a supporter of the pre-Columbian cause, D. J. M. Wright, diagnosed syphilis in Stone Age remains. He based his finding on lumps (called bossing) on the cranium, plus some pitting on the bones at the back and sides of the skull, and a relatively depressed nasal bridge. In addition, he said that worn molar teeth showing taurodontism – large broad crowns and very short roots – resembled the so-called mulberry molars that are an indication of syphilis. Wright also described a bow-shaped thighbone, declaring it was evidence of syphilitic osteitis. In the end it was shown that many of the apparently pathological lesions Wright had found were nothing more than biomechanical differences between the skeletons of Stone Age man and modern human beings.

Adding to the vigorous argument in this area, another controversy centres on the four diseases caused by bacteria of the genus *Treponema*. The question the debate focuses on is this: are venereal syphilis, endemic syphilis, pinta and yaws really different diseases, caused by subordinate treponemal bacteria, or are they just different-looking infections caused by one species of bacteria, *Treponema pallidum*? If they really are separate afflictions, then as a group they can be given the clinical title treponematoses. If, on the other hand, they are merely different ways of the same disease revealing itself, then the name for the infection will be treponematosis.

Both endemic and venereal syphilis are conventionally attributed to *Treponema pallidum*; pinta is blamed on *Treponema carateum*, and the species believed to cause yaws is called *Treponema pertenue*. It is this very distinction of sub-species that has been investigated. The fact is that all three are identical in appearance and in their chemical characteristics; they are indistinguishable by any known laboratory test. From the point of view of immunology, a variety of alterations to the blood of individuals infected with all three bacterial strains are identical too. This evidence has convinced prominent investigators, notably E. H. Hudson, that only one species of the genus *Treponema* causes these infections – *Treponema pallidum.*

That premise has its opponents. They point to the different clinical features of the three diseases and to their clearly defined distribution in the world. The bacteria, they say, are obviously three distinct species. Neither of the arguments has been convincingly defeated, and probably will not be until there are further developments in the equipment used for bacterial testing, or until significant advances are made in the way that bacteriologists work.

But while aspects of treponemal bacterial identity are still in question, the clinical features of the four infections are no mystery at all, and they have been known for a long time. The changes caused by venereal syphilis, endemic syphilis, pinta and yaws, as seen with the naked eye and through the microscope, are absolutely identical. Any differences between them are solely differences of greater or lesser severity; there are no variations of characteristic. However, because pinta produces pathological alteration only in the skin, there are grounds for arguing that it is different. Since pinta has no effect on the skeleton, its traces never appear on bones at archaeological digs. Another feature that makes pinta arguably different from the other three diseases is that it has never been used successfully to inoculate laboratory animals, whereas inoculation of animals can easily be done with the others. Also, the severely debilitating and deadly effects produced by the tertiary phases of venereal syphilis, endemic syphilis and yaws do not occur in pinta.

Further investigation of that intriguing mystery is stalled. It seems clear to some investigators that on the evidence as it stands we are witnessing the process of evolution at work in *Treponema pallidum*. If that is the case, it could mean that the treponemal diseases will change, or multiply in number, or grow more virulent, or do all three. Disease has a way of finding ways around humanity's barriers, and a number of serious diseases kept in check by penicillin for nearly sixty years have recently begun to show resistance. There is no reason to assume that the treponemal infections would behave any differently.

For those supporting the pre-Columbian hypothesis, hope of proving their point came in 1994 from the north of England. A new courthouse had been planned for the town of Kingston upon Hull. The court was to be built over the known remains of a medieval Augustinian friary, although in the end a car park was erected there. Once the remains of the previous buildings had been removed and the ground had been cleared, a full-scale excavation was launched. The finds, as they accumulated, proved more and more enlightening as the days went by.

In England, Augustinian or Austin friars were one of the lesser orders during the Middle Ages, and only forty of their houses were set up in England and Wales. The Hull house was established in 1316 or 1317, and it accommodated up to eighteen friars at any one time. It remained occupied until 1539, and was the very last dwelling of the Augustinian order to surrender to the Crown at the Dissolution.

Archaeological investigation has been carried out on very few of the Augustinian houses, and until this excavation hardly anything of the physical form or layout of the establishment was known. In spite of Second World War bomb damage and extensive building over the monastic complex throughout the centuries, the surviving medieval features were remarkably good, and in some areas they were even classi-fied as excellent. The excavation covered 2,070 square metres and remains the biggest excavation ever undertaken in the region.

As time passed, archaeologists and historians connected with the excavation built up a comprehensive picture of life in the old port. Alongside the emerging image of the medieval town, a clearer understanding of the daily routines of the friars of Hull also began to emerge.

In the Roman Catholic Church, an Augustinian was a member of any of the religious orders of men and women who based their constitutions on the *Rule of St Augustine*, a volume of instructions on the religious life written by the great Western theologian, Augustine, and widely disseminated after his death in aad 430. More specifically, the name 'Augustinian' is used to designate members of two main branches of the order, Augustinian Canons and Augustinian Hermits, with their female offshoots.

The Augustinian Hermits, or Austin Friars, were one of the four mendicant (begging) orders of the Middle Ages. They lived by whatever others provided, but they were industrious nevertheless and provided a considerable number of important services, both clerical and medical. In the year 428 they were dispersed by the Vandal invasion of northern Africa. A number of congregations of hermits who had been following the *Rule of St Augustine* went on to found monasteries in central and northern Italy, where they stayed independent of one another until 1244, when Pope Innocent IV conglomerated them into a single order. In 1256 Pope Alexander IV called them out of their life of seclusion and into the cities, where they were to become active lay propagators of their faith. The order spread quickly across Europe, and soon they were taking a leading part in the life of universities and centres of ecclesiastical affairs. Perhaps the most famous Augustinian friar of all was the Protestant reformer Martin Luther.

Working from their dispensary, where they compounded their own medicines, the friars of Hull tended the very poor of the town – sailors, prostitutes, tenement dwellers – and treated them for a range of diseases and afflictions that nowadays are hardly ever encountered. The rich people, who were the merchants and business owners of the port, paid to be buried in the friary grounds and to have masses said for their souls.

The Hull friars left evidence in the ground of their active and varied lives. They were literate, and they enjoyed music; they went on pilgrimages to Spain, and there is even evidence that some of them went as far as Palestine. They had trading connections all the way across Europe, from Lithuania and Poland to France and Spain. They ate well, probably too well for their own good, and they drank vast amounts of ale and the finest claret. They had flexible wooden rods buried with them in their coffins, suggesting to some observers that they may have gone in for occasional mortification of the flesh, perhaps as a moral counterbalance to their excessive eating and drinking. Most interesting and revealing of all at the excavation site were the 245 well-preserved skeletons, 207 of them relatively complete. Several show signs of DISH (diffuse idiopathic skeletal hyperostosis), a painful thickening and stiffening of the spine caused by a high-fat diet and a sedentary way of life.

To historians of disease, however, there was one dominant and arresting feature among the friary skeletons that they felt might change the history books: some of the bones appeared to show signs of syphilis.

Palaeopathology is the science of locating and demonstrating signs of disease in ancient human and animal remains. It is the science that would be brought to bear in the Hull excavation to determine whether the suspect bones really had been affected by syphilis.

Palaeopathology is never an easy or uncontroversial science to practise, and when it comes to finding traces of treponemal disease in ancient skeletal remains, the possibilities for error and controversy multiply sharply.

The difficulty is not eased by the fact that evidence is distinctly thin on the ground. For a start, because pinta does not affect the skeleton, traces of the infection have never survived from antiquity. Overall, the fact is that fewer than fifteen per cent of individuals infected with treponemal infections ever show bone changes from their disease. The number of cases with bone damage that can be identified and classified goes from between three and five per cent of all cases of yaws, to between ten and twelve per cent of all cases of venereal syphilis. Endemic syphilis comes somewhere between the two.

The bone changes that *are* found in venereal syphilis, endemic syphilis and yaws are mainly the legacy of osteomyelitis – inflammation of the bone marrow – which results in gross bone destruction accompanied by signs of fairly extensive bone regrowth and certain very specific microscopic features.

In yaws the tibia is the bone most often affected. The skull is less often involved, but when it is the degree of damage and destruction is usually much worse than in syphilis, especially in the nose and mouth areas. There are usually irregular crater depressions on the surface of the skull, but on occasion the degree of destruction is truly widespread. That is the case in the condition called gangosa, considered to be a true consequence of yaws, where destructive ulceration begins on the soft palate and extends on to the hard palate and upwards into the region behind – and communicating with – the nose, mouth and larynx, resulting in destruction of the whole of the victim's nasal area and upper jaw. Further mutilation is caused by extensive scarring and destruction of much of the flesh of the face, a result that can be more devastating than the worst mutilations of leprosy. The osteomyelitis of the tibia is more common, though, and quite distinctive. Because of its peculiar shape, it is often called a sabre shin.

Damage to the skull in endemic syphilis is about as uncommon as it is in yaws, but when it does occur it can completely destroy the nasal area and the whole upper jaw. As in infection with yaws, the tibia is the bone most often affected, resulting again in the characteristic sabre shape. The differences between yaws and endemic syphilis are seen in their earlier stages and their individual geographic preferences. They are both common and endemic in hot climates, but yaws appears to be partial to the humid tropics, while endemic syphilis prevails in hotter, parched regions.

Like endemic syphilis and yaws, the long bone most often affected in venereal syphilis is the tibia, which becomes deformed with osteomyelitis. Even so, only ten or twelve per cent of venereal syphilitics suffer *any* changes in *any* of their bones. Since the only evidence of syphilis in ancient times is gained from skeletal remains, it follows that the profusion of the disease in early times could be underestimated by as much as ninety per cent. Venereal syphilis can also cause destructive changes in joints, most commonly the knee. The infection may be centred on the knee itself, or affect the knee later in the progress of the disease. The joint often becomes damaged by a complex involvement of the nervous system which also robs the knee of any feeling; this is called a Charcot's joint, and is another clearly definable sign of syphilis in ancient bones. In contrast to endemic syphilis and yaws, however, the skull is commonly involved in venereal syphilis, and the changes in that region usually confirm a diagnosis. The bones of the vault of the skull show a highly typical worm-eaten look that has been given the name *caries sicca*. The inflammation starts in the interior structure of the bones and spreads gradually outwards and inwards. Sometimes the skull perforates. The picture an investigator usually sees is one of gross destruction and, here and there, patchy regrowth of bone. Changes occur in the nasal area and on the palate, but not so conspicuously as they do in endemic syphilis and yaws.

So what did the investigators learn about the suspect bones at the Hull excavation? Not as much as they had hoped. There were difficulties over dating the remains, and in any case only one skeleton was involved: it showed possibly syphilitic signs on a shin, and what looked like the presence of *caries sicca* on the skull. Charlotte Roberts, a palaeopathologist who holds to the pre-Columbian theory, said that when she saw the skeleton from the Hull dig, the first thing that grabbed her attention was the skull. She was convinced she was looking at a case of syphilis. 'It's classic,' she said. 'It's what you see in books that show you how the disease affects the skeleton. It was just so convincing.'

Dr Bruce Rothschild, on the other hand, is always wary of conclusions that are drawn on the basis of small samples. 'As soon as you start examining bones and you find that one in ten individuals in the population have the disease but not more than that,' he said, 'you're already at a frequency that's too low for yaws and it helps you to recognise that it's likely to be syphilis. But you can't use just one sign, just as you can't use one bone – and just as you can't use one skeleton.'

George Armalegos is deeply sceptical of the Hull discovery. He does not believe this is evidence of pre-Columbian syphilis, nor does he believe that the other isolated examples found in the Old World are syphilis, either. He has cast an expert's eye across many skeletons over many years; his conviction has hardened with time and experience. 'There's a huge amount of evidence in the New World, and nothing convincing in the Old World,' he says flatly.

Part of the issue is the paucity of evidence. So *little* evidence occurs before 1492. For example in Czechoslovakia they looked at ten thousand skeletons and found no trace of syphilis before 1492, but incredible numbers after 1492. Japan, no evidence until contact occurs after 1500 – India, the same thing. What does that tell me?

Controversy will continue, and new questions will be raised. Aside from the Columbian and pre-Columbian arguments, the treponemal diseases themselves still raise perplexing questions. Why does pinta not affect the skeleton, and why can't it be used to infect laboratory animals? Why is syphilis the only syndrome to produce congenital disease? Are there three species of bacteria subordinate to *Treponema pallidum*, or is it the solitary cause of venereal syphilis, endemic syphilis, pinta and yaws?

Whether or not syphilis existed in Europe before Columbus returned from America, continued research into the long history of the disease remains an important research objective. Given the enthusiasm of expert investigators on both sides of the controversy, intensive analysis of Old World bones must, eventually, uncover a decisive answer.

BIBLIOGRAPHY

BLOOD RED ROSES

The Battle of Towton by
A. W. Boardman; Alan Sutton
Publishing, 1994

The Wars of the Roses by Charles Ross;
Thames & Hudson, 1986

The Medieval Archer by Jim Bradbury;
Boydell Press, 1985

Medieval Warfare ed. Maurice Keen;
Oxford University Press, 1999

War in the Middle Ages by Philippe
Contamine and M. Jones;
Blackwell, 1986

Medieval England by Edmund King;
Phaidon Press, 1988

*Blood Red Roses: The Archaeology of a
Mass Grave from the Battle of Towton* AD
1461 ed. Veronica Fiorato, Anthea
Bolyston and Christopher Knusel;
Oxbow Books, 2000

CANYON CANNIBALS

Man Corn by Christy G. Turner and
Jacqueline A. Turner; University
of Utah Press (US), 1999

In Search of the Old Ones by David
Roberts; Touchstone Press (US), 1997

Roads to the Centre Place by Kathryn
Gabriel; Johnson Books (US), 1991

A History of Latin America, Volume 1
by Benjamin Keen; Houghton Mifflin,
1992

People of Chaco by Kendrick Frazier;
W. W. Norton & Co (US), 1999

THE LOST VIKINGS

A History of the Vikings by Gwyn
Jones; Oxford University Press, 1984

Cultural Atlas of the Viking World by J. G.
Campbell et al; Facts on File, 1994

The Vinland Sagas ed. Magnus
Magnusson and H. Pallson;
Penguin, 1965

Viking by Magnus Magnusson; Orbis,
1976

BEWITCHED

Poisons of the Past by Mary Kilbourne
Matossian;
Yale University Press, 1991

The Devil's Disciples by Peter Charles
Hoffer; Johns Hopkins
University Press (US), 1996

Ergotism: the Satan Loosed in Salem? by
Linnda R. Caporael; *Science*, vol. 192,
April 1976

The Story of Ergot by F. J. Bove; Barger
(US), 1970

Ergot ed. Vladimik Kren and Ladislav
Cvak; Harwood Academic (US), 1999

THE SYPHILIS ENIGMA

History of Syphilis by Claude Quetel;
Polity Press, 1992

The Great Pox by J. Arrizabalaga
et al; Yale University Press, 1997

Syphilis in Shakespeare's England by
Johannes Fabricius; Jessica Kingsley
Publishers, 1994

The Archaeology of Disease by C.
Roberts and K. Manchester;
Alan Sutton Publishing, 1995

The Tuskegee Syphilis Study by Fred D.
Gray; Black Belt Press (US), 1998

Bad Blood by James H. Jones; Free
Press (US), 1993

INDEX

PICTURE CREDITS

Page 1: Matt Griggs/UNP.

Page 2 (top): Trinity College, Cambridge; (bottom): Matt Griggs/UNP.

Page 3 (top): Liz Hymans/CORBIS; (bottom): Meoduff Everton/
CORBIS.

Page 4 (top): Engel Brothers Media Inc; (middle): Engel Brothers
Media Inc; (bottom): The Greenland Museum, 1988.

Page 5 (top): The National Museum of Denmark; (bottom):
Ted Spiegel/CORBIS.

Page 6 (top): Wolfgang Kaehler/CORBIS; (bottom left): Forhistorisk
Museum, Denmark/Munoz-Yague/Science Photo Library; (bottom
right): Astrid & Hanns-Frieder Michler/Science Photo Library.

Page 7 (top): Mary Evans Picture Library; (bottom):
Bettmann/CORBIS.

Page 8 (top left): Mary Evans Picture Library; (top right):
Alfred Pasieka/Science Photo Library; (bottom): Mary Evans/Explorer.